A Daughter's Gift of Love

A HOLOCAUST MEMOIR BY TRUDI BIRGER

A
Daughter's
Gift
of Love

A HOLOCAUST MEMOIR BY TRUDI BIRGER

written with Jeffrey M. Green

THE
JEWISH
PUBLICATION
SOCIETY
Philadelphia
Jerusalem
5753–1992

Originally published in German under the title
Im Angesicht des Feuers

Copyright © 1990 R. Piper GmbH & Co. KG., Munich, Germany

This edition copyright © 1992 by
Trudi Birger and Jeffrey M. Green
First English edition   All rights reserved
Manufactured in the United States of America

Library of Congress Cataloging in Publication Data

Birger, Trudi.
[Im Angesicht des Feuers.   English]
A dauther's gift of love : a Holocaust memoir / by Trudi Birger,
written with Jeffrey M. Green.
p.   cm.
Translation of: Im Angesicht des Feuers.
Summary: The author, a survivor of the Holocaust,
describes her ordeal of being held with her mother
in the concentration camp at Stutthof.
ISBN 0-8276-0420-3
1. Birger, Trudi.
2. Holocaust, Jewish (1939-1945)—Personal narratives.
3. Jews—Lithuania—Kaunas—Persecutions.
4. Kaunas (Lithuania)—Ethnic relations.
[1. Holocaust, Jewish (1939-1945)—Personal narratives.
2. Birger, Trudi.]
I. Green, Jeffrey M.   II. Title.
D804.3.B55   1992
940.53′18—dc20   92-15503
                                    CIP
                                    AC

Designed by Arlene Putterman

DEDICATION

This book is dedicated to my dear husband, Zeev, who has been my constant companion in every kind of circumstance; to my eldest son, Doron, who often asked questions about my dreadful past in the camps, and to his wife, Aya; to my second son, Oded, who always showed solidarity with my suffering, and to his wife, Nurit; and to my youngest son, Gili, who always listened to my story with particular interest and empathy, and to his wife, Diti.

My sons never knew their maternal grandfather, who was killed in the Kovno ghetto for trying to hide a group of children under the roof of the Jewish Committee; nor did they know Zeev's parents or his brother, who were all killed by the Nazis. This book was written in honor of their memory.

Finally, I also dedicate this book to my wonderful grandchildren, Adi, Eran, Tal, Liron, Ori, and Shachar. I am grateful to have lived to see my story preserved and passed on to coming generations. My dear grandchildren, when you are old enough to read and understand this book, may it keep alive the memory of your grandparents and the millions of other Jews who underwent this horrible experience, most of whom were not fortunate enough to survive.

I am grateful to my coauthor, Jeffrey Green, for his sensitive understanding of my Holocaust story. During the past forty years I never found a non-Holocaust survivor to whom I could talk so freely. Jeffrey listened to me with full understanding for hundreds of hours. There were many moments when tears filled his eyes, his expression was sad, and his face turned pale. We had to interrupt our conversation, and often it was hard to resume. Jeffrey sometimes tried to spare me pain by not asking pressing questions, but on the contrary, I asked him not to be too sensitive with me. This was the only way to write the book. The long months writing with him proved one of the greatest experiences in my life.

I hope my story will be read by children and adults, so that no one in the world will be able to forget the dreadful fate of the six million innocent Jews who couldn't survive. I keep asking myself: Where was justice?

Trudi Birger

FOREWORD

This is the story of a unique human being: Trudi Birger, a survivor of the Nazi death camps, perhaps the only person in the world to be plucked out of a crowd of doomed people just before they were thrown into the crematorium at the Stutthof concentration camp. Trudi was saved from death dozens of times—by her will to live, her quick wit, her self-confidence, and, especially, her love for her mother.

Although Trudi survived physically, the Holocaust destroyed the substance of her entire life, past, present, and future. She was cut off from childhood roots and the environment from which she sprang: the Orthodox Jewish community of Frankfurt, Germany, a refined, cultivated, wealthy, honorable home. She lost all of the constants in a child's life. In addition, her expectations, hopes, and ambitions were all wiped away.

Any survivor's story is necessarily incredible, because the odds against survival were so huge. Trudi's story is one of courage, faith, ingenuity, and determined hope—and a series of miracles. It is also a story of self-sacrifice and loss, and of the constant love between a mother and her daughter: Trudi's devotion to her mother and her mother's devotion to her are truly what kept them both alive.

The purpose of this book is not simply to recount facts, which are, after all, readily available, but rather to recount personal experience, to tell what it is like to be the person who has had these experiences. Although it may appear that Trudi now is living a normal, happy, and productive life in Jerusalem, is such a life really possible for a Holocaust survivor? Today Trudi is driven by a sense of purpose, the desire to be useful to others. She donates vast amounts of time and energy to exemplary volunteer work to help the poor. This book is another outgrowth of her sense of mission, the mission of a survivor.

Here is a brief outline of Trudi's dramatic life. She was born in Frankfurt, Germany, in 1927. Her family fled to the free port city of Memel on the Baltic Sea, in 1933, after the Nazi takeover in Germany. They had to flee again, to Lithuania, in 1938, after the Nazis seized Memel. Trudi and her family lived under Soviet rule in Kovno from 1939 to 1941. Then the Nazis invaded and confined them in the Kovno ghetto, where they lived from 1941 to 1944. Trudi's father was killed on his birthday, March 28, 1944, for trying to conceal children during the notorious *Kinderaktion* (Children's Action). When the ghetto was liquidated, Trudi and her mother were sent to the Stutthof concentration camp and then to labor camps (1944 – 45). After the liberation, Trudi and her mother were repatriated to Germany, where Trudi married. Then Trudi, her husband, and her mother all moved to Israel.

Jeffrey M. Green, the coauthor, was born and raised in Greenwich Village, New York City, and graduated Princeton University summa cum laude in French. He went on to graduate school at Harvard University, earning a doctorate in comparative literature, before deciding to move to Israel with his family. He has lived in Israel since 1973, where he works as a translator (he has translated several novels by Aharon Appelfeld) and free-lance writer. A short afterword written in his own name and voice concludes the book.

CONTENTS

11

Alone with Mother

CHAPTER ONE

My mother and I reluctantly inched forward in the long, ragged line of silent women. We were two lonely creatures among hundreds, perhaps thousands, of women that morning, crowded together under the vicious, indifferent gaze of our guards—how many vast crowds of women had they processed so far?—in a hostile, open space, dressed in castoffs, with rough wooden clogs on our feet and faces blanked by fear. Here were no smiles, no flashes of recognition, no nods of encouragement, nothing but the empty dullness of dread.

Most of the women looked at the packed earth beneath their feet, trodden down by the anonymous multitudes who had been herded through this place before us, human lives reduced to a tiny packet of fear and resignation. Each of us, with no one to help us, was on line to have her fortune told and carried out immediately, to be sent to life or to death. It was late in the war, and we knew what to expect from the Nazis.

Not all the women who had come with us in the train from the Kovno ghetto had been strangers, but now we were mingled with women from all over Europe, women separated from one another by language—not that we tried to speak to one another—and isolated by fright.

There were no friends or relatives to support us. Only my mother and I were left clinging to each other. My father and my uncle had been shot. My mother's parents and her surviving brother had chosen to hide in a bunker when the Germans liquidated the Kovno ghetto, in the hope that the Russians would get there before the Nazis routed them out and killed them. We didn't know whether or not they had survived, and years were to pass before we learned the dreadful truth. No one bothered to tell us the rules of the game or to help us work out the odds. How was anyone to know what the right decision was?

We were forced to make life-and-death choices in darkness. Even I, a mere child, had already made such choices any number of times.

Three days before, at the railroad depot in Kovno, there had been brutal confusion and panic. The soldiers made everything move very fast. They didn't give us time to take stock of our situation or to say goodbye to our loved ones. Throngs of soldiers shouted orders at us, pushed us from one place to another, forced us apart. From their point of view it might have been well organized. Without warning, they separated the men from the women and put thousands of us onto trains in a few short hours. That's when Mother and I lost contact with my older brother Manfred—just before they loaded us onto the trains.

The Nazis made us leave the Kovno ghetto without any belongings except the clothes on our backs. When we arrived at the concentration camp, they herded us into a huge shed and made us strip, and they took away the clothes and shoes we had been wearing on the train. These clothes may have been tattered and soiled from three years of wear in the ghetto, and filthy from our ride in the crowded cattle cars, but at least they had been ours. Now nothing at all of our own was left, not one of the meager possessions we had managed to keep in the ghetto, not even a pin for our hair. Now we wore coarse wooden clogs and clothes that the Nazi guards had given us, second-, third-, or fourthhand civilian clothes with yellow stars sewn on the back, not striped camp uniforms like those worn by the Polish Gentile prisoners whom we could see on the other side of the barbed wire, the frightening, savage criminals who maintained the camp.

It was a sunny, warm July morning in 1944. We had been caged in the densely packed railroad cars for three days, with almost nothing to eat. Yet despite hunger, fatigue, and fear, despite the humiliation of being stripped, of having a number scratched onto my arm, of being ordered about by the uniformed Kapos, with their switches whistling menacingly at their sides—despite all that, the sun and the fresh air gave me some energy. I was a just a girl of sixteen, thin and physically immature, but despite all the years of privation, somehow I still had a store of youthful vitality.

We inched forward in that dense line of strangers, where no one wanted to move forward, toward the point where we would be thrown from one realm of doubt to another. We were forced forward by the crush of women behind us, harried along by the Kapos with their switches and by the guards who stood along the barbed wire fence with their dogs. Tall, stark watchtowers manned by soldiers with machine guns loomed against the sun on the perimeter of the camp.

I heard the guards and their dogs snarling. The women shuffled forward with barely a sound, only moans and sighs of fear, weeping, whispered prayers. The northern summer sun sparkled on the soldiers' buttons and on their guns, polished leather boots, and brass buckles. It glinted in their narrowed eyes as they watched us. Huge dogs strained at their leashes, panting and baring their teeth. Could they smell our fear the way I could, the acrid, dried sweat on our bodies after days of not washing, the reek of urine and feces that we couldn't clean off, our breath foul with disease, hunger, tooth decay, fear? My mother and I clung to each other. All the women huddled close together for the illusion of protection, though we were strangers.

Now not many women stood between us and the doctor in charge of the selection. All my attention focused on him. He was going to decide my fate in a moment. He was a tall, handsome, blond man in a Nazi uniform. He stood his ground proudly at the end of the line, marking the center of that fragment of the universe. He looked intently and impersonally at each woman as she stood before him, inspecting her for flaws that would make her useless as a laborer. With small, cold gestures, barely a word, he sent some to the left, others to the right. There wasn't one of us who didn't know what that meant.

I was fascinated by that handsome, well-fed doctor, such a tall, clean, graceful man. His face was intelligent and aloof, not vicious. Perhaps, if I smiled pleasantly at him, he would do what I hoped he would do. My mother and I drew closer. For myself, I wasn't concerned about his verdict. I knew I would pass. I had had plenty of practice at making it through selections. I had learned how to look cheerful and stand as straight as I could, to show that I was full of energy and goodwill. But I wasn't sure about my mother. She wasn't even forty, but she had never been a particularly vigorous woman. She had developed a heart condition as a child, and my father had always pampered her. Until we were driven out of our home and into the ghetto, he had always stood between her and the harsh realities of the world. Even in the ghetto she had looked to him for protection. But the Nazis had murdered him, and since that tragic loss, only a few months ago, my mother had aged drastically. She looked closer to sixty than to forty. Her skin was wrinkled and gray, her eyes had no sparkle. And the dress they had given her at the camp, a shapeless black thing, did nothing to make her look younger. This was my mother, who had worn only the finest hand-sewn clothing when I was a child. Now she looked like a listless beggar-woman.

Before we were put on the trains at Kovno we had been a little hopeful. The Germans were emptying the ghetto. Couldn't there possibly be a change for the better? The Russians weren't far away. The Germans were clearly, though too slowly, losing the war. Perhaps the Germans had some reason to keep us alive until the end of the war. No one had told us where we were going or what to expect.

Within minutes we had all lost hope. They stuffed us into sealed cattle cars. It was inhumanly crowded, hot and stuffy. Women were screaming, gasping, and fainting. They didn't give us any food, but there was water to drink from rusty metal containers, which we called *paklashkes*. The ride lasted three days that felt like three years. It was an erratic journey to nowhere, sometimes fast, sometimes slow, sometimes stationary. It didn't seem as if the Germans knew what to do with us. That was frightening. But I supported my mother by pretending to be optimistic.

At one point they opened the doors and stationed guards in all the cars. They kept warning us over loud-speakers: "Anyone who tries to jump out of the train will be shot down on the spot." We heard shots, but we couldn't tell whether someone had really tried to leap off the train, or whether the guards were just trying to intimidate us. They kept cursing us, calling us dirty sows.

I got as close as I could to the open doors as we rode. At night the guards got drowsy. Sometimes the train slowed down and we passed through forests. The trees grew right next to the tracks. If you were daring, you could leap out and vanish among the trees before the guards had a chance to shoot. Here and there, beyond the trees, I could see houses. Perhaps someone living there would have mercy on us. The Russians were approaching.

I stood near the open door with my mother. "Let's jump," I whispered to her.

"I can't," she said. "You jump."

She was right. She was too weak to jump. She didn't have the courage to run away into the woods. I couldn't leave her, and I couldn't pull her out of the train with me. I swore to myself yet again that we would live together or die together.

She urged me to jump. She even tried to push me. But she wasn't strong enough.

When the train stopped, we didn't know where we were. It was Stutthof, a place not far from Danzig, on the Baltic coast. The Nazis disguised the nature of the camp from the outside. A small band of uniformed Gentile musicians greeted us with music in the open area between the gray cement wall of the camp and the railroad plat-form. At first I couldn't help feeling hopeful again. Per-haps this was a kind of transit camp where we could wait out the war until the Russians advanced and liberated us.

The camp was isolated. A tall stone wall outside the camp hid its true character. The landscape was flat and wooded. The guards herded us through a big gate, and we immediately understood where we were. We saw the elec-trified barbed wire fence, and the brutal criminals and political prisoners in striped uniforms who stood on the other side. It was a gigantic place. You couldn't take it all in with your eyes. It seemed to go on and on indefinitely. All our illusions evaporated. Smoke rose from tall chim-neys. I imagined it was a bakery or a factory. I had not yet heard of the crematoria.

Masses of Jewish women crammed through the gates, driven forward toward a huge hangar where Kapos scratched numbers into our arms, drawing blood. The women who marked us enjoyed making it hurt. They lashed out at us with whips, almost at random, beating us for the pleasure of it. We had to strip and put on the clothes they gave us. My mother got a shapeless black dress, and I received a blue skirt and a red blouse.

Now my mother and I stood before the doctor. His eyes penetrated our clothes, found our weaknesses: "The old woman to the left. The girl to the right." I didn't move. I stood and watched exactly where my mother was sent, through the gate, to the other side of the fence, toward some long wooden barracks standing not too far off. I didn't move, but the Kapos shoved me out of the way, toward a column of women lined up in rows of six. This was the work formation. In a moment we would be marched off somewhere to do forced labor. I had never been absolutely alone before. The other women stood passively, waiting for whatever would come. But I couldn't accept what had happened to me.

For three years, from the summer of 1941 until the summer of 1944, I had done forced labor for the Nazis, but always alongside my mother. We had always watched over each other and sacrificed ourselves for each other—literally. Every morning at seven we had lined up at the gates of the ghetto, and they had marched us out to our workplace. Most of the time my mother and I had worked in the Kriegslazarett, a military hospital that took care of wounded German soldiers. Our job was cleaning the bathrooms and toilets, the filthiest work they could find for us. At least we had been together. My mother had watched over me.

But I didn't need her to take care of me now. I knew I had to take care of myself. Father had been killed on March 28, 1944, his forty-seventh birthday, during the *Aktion*, when the Germans had rounded up all the children remaining in the ghetto and killed them. Father tried to save a large group of children by hiding them under the roof of the Jewish Committee building where he worked, but the Germans found them, took them to the Ninth Fort on a hill outside the city, and shot them all with machine guns, including my father. We heard what had happened from witnesses.

He didn't have to die then. He didn't have to make a futile effort to save children who were doomed anyway.

But that was so typical of my father, a man who always thought of other people first.

His death devastated my mother, but somehow, despite my grief, I forced myself to remain hopeful, even though there was no hope. Until Father died, together they had encouraged each other and hid their fears from me, insulating me as much as they could from the horrors of the ghetto. We did whatever we could to stay together and keep up our hopes in a situation where there was no reason to think we might survive. After Father was gone, my mother couldn't hide her despair from me. I had to be the strong one, to make sure she ate whatever there was to eat, to make sure she didn't give up, and to pretend that I expected a miracle, that the Russians would come soon and drive away the Nazis.

From my place in the column of laborers I quickly sized up the situation. Women rapidly filled in behind me, relatively strong young women. I could see the camp gate in front of us and a train waiting to take us away. In a moment they would march us out of the gate, to the train, and I would never see my mother again. I strained to look through the wire fence and see where she had gone. On the other side of the fence the weak, older women weren't lined up in columns. They were milling about near the barracks, and the Kapos were ignoring them. All their attention was concentrated on the selection point, where the handsome, blond doctor was sending people right or left. I thought I saw my mother in her black dress, staggering around the corner of a barrack. It was impossible, but I had to get to her.

In the ghetto I had always been a resourceful girl. I still

wonder where that resourcefulness came from. I wasn't a street urchin, used to living by my wits in a hostile world, shifting for myself because I was neglected. On the contrary, I had been pampered as a child. In Frankfurt, where I was born, I had had a nanny, a registered nurse, who wore a nurse's cap with a red Star of David on her forehead. What an irony, now that I think of it! Our Gentile nurse had proudly worn what came to be the symbol of our persecution. She saw to our every need. My brother and I were among the best-dressed children in Frankfurt. Even after we fled Frankfurt and my father was no longer as wealthy as he had been, he still made a good living, and I was raised with every comfort he could afford.

Before the war began, when we were living in Memel, a port city on the Baltic coast, north of Stutthof, I used to dress up in organdy gowns and patent leather shoes, and my aunt Tita would take me to tea dances. She ordered hot chocolate for me, and I would perform waltzes and tangos with the twelve-year-old boys. I treasured the memory of that hot chocolate, and I dreamt of it night after night. I decided that the first thing I would do after the war would be to drink a cup of rich, hot chocolate.

Perhaps the change in me wasn't all that surprising, as I think harder about it. My upbringing was privileged, but Father never let me forget that with privilege comes responsibility. German Jews are known to take an earnest approach to life, and we were an Orthodox household, so our lives were doubly defined by duties and obligations. We had high standards of behavior to meet, even when we were well off.

I quickly learned how to manage in the ghetto. My

parents sewed secret pockets in my clothes, and I smuggled food into the ghetto for the elderly people who couldn't work. Nazi guards inspected us at the gates, but I forced myself to smile and hide my fear, and they let me through. I was always ready to take chances. I trusted my luck and my wits.

I also liked to take charge of things, when I could. In the ghetto, when they still let us buy supplies, I baked bread for everyone. We got a bucket full of flour. This was still in the beginning, when Jews could buy things for money and ration tickets.

First, I left a bit of flour in water overnight to start a sourdough. Then I mixed the dough and kneaded it. I have a very clear memory of kneading that bucket full of dough. I was barely thirteen and small for my age. One of the neighbors said, "You're so little, your arm barely reaches to the bottom of the bucket." But I was proud to be baking for everyone. We had an old oven in our quarters. I got it to work and baked the bread all by myself. It came out well. People called me "the baker-girl."

Who could imagine that after a couple of years in the ghetto, when food became scarce, fresh-baked bread made from real flour would be such a delicacy that, despite modesty and strict Jewish morals, some mothers would be willing to send their daughters to sleep with a Nazi guard just to get some?

Another time we got some carrots, and I made a carrot cake. We needed the natural sugar. I put myself in charge of the baking, and I did the job well. I treasure that image I have of myself, a small, blond girl, arms up to her shoulders in a bucket of dough. That was the girl who survived the war, not the cute little child in patent leather shoes and an organdy dress, doing ballroom dances in a tearoom in Memel.

Now I had to be resourceful again, more resourceful and determined than I had ever been in my life. I was going to get to my mother, no matter what. I noticed an unguarded gate in the electrified fence ahead of me. I sneaked forward from my line of six women to the one in front of me, throwing off the count. Then I moved forward again, to the next line. The other women stood passively, dazed from the train trip and immobilized by the shock of arrival in Stutthof, by the danger of the selection, and by the relief of being sent to the right, to life—and perhaps also by grief at being separated from their loved ones. We all looked the same in our cast-off clothes. I pushed forward to another row, moving to the side, toward the gate.

Now the guards noticed the disorder. The row I left had only five women in it. The row I was standing in had seven women, but by now I was four or five rows ahead of the row I had left. The guards didn't know where to look for me. They moved toward the row of five with their dogs, and I moved forward again. Now I was standing near the gate. Somehow I knew immediately how to get through, just where to touch the catch so I wouldn't be shocked by the electrified wire. The guards were shouting, ordering a count, looking for the missing woman. I reached up to the catch and let myself through the gate.

Now I was on the side of the doomed. The guards and their dogs saw me running, but they couldn't break through the line of women to catch me. I raced forward and mingled with a group of women. We all looked the same. There was no way of picking me out to punish me. Anyway, I was on the side where everyone was going to be sent to the gas chambers. That was punishment enough.

On the dead side of the fence they let the prisoners mill around until the day's selection was finished. It wasn't like the strict order on the other side, where they lined the women up and promptly marched them off to be transported to labor camps. They had no use for the women on the dead side before they killed them, except to beat them when the Kapos felt like it. There were rows of stark, unpainted, wooden barracks where the Nazis crowded the women together and half starved them to death before they gassed them.

I had seen my mother disappear behind one of the barracks. I rushed ahead to try to find her. I didn't really notice the other women, except to see that they weren't my mother. Each of them, hundreds and hundreds of lonely, feeble, grief-stricken women, was on her way to certain death. How could anyone look at them? Such staggering sorrow was massed together there. Where was my mother? I called to woman after woman, looked at face after face, seeing emptiness and dread but not my mother's lovely features. "I'm not your mother," some of them answered me.

As a young woman Mother had been known as "*die schoene* Rosel," beautiful Rose. That hadn't been so long ago, but it was in another lifetime. While in her late twenties and early thirties she had always dressed with exquisite taste. Her clothes were all handmade, modest but fashionable, with appliqué and fancy stitching. Her brown hair was always done perfectly. The smell of her perfume was the smell of my childhood. Her graceful hands as she played piano were the embodiment of delicacy, skill, and purpose. She was a cultured, well-read woman, certainly better versed in German literature and music than were the brutal Aryan guards in Stutthof. Despite her youth, my mother had been a leader among the women of the Orthodox community of Frankfurt. She had organized a charity kindergarten. Even in the ghetto she had managed to retain her grace and dignity. I might find my mother, but I would never find the woman she once had been.

Then incredibly, among all those lost souls, I spotted her. She was knotting a stocking around her neck, preparing to strangle herself. I couldn't believe my eyes. I rushed forward and called to her.

"Rosel!" I called. "Mother!"

But she didn't answer me. She was appalled to see me. She didn't want to recognize me as her daughter.

"Mother," I called again.

"I'm not your mother," she said. She wanted to die alone. But I took the stocking from around her neck.

"My child," she said, finally acknowledging my presence and speaking with the old, elegant, literary formality I remembered so well, "you have come into death." I knew it. But it didn't matter. Without her, I was dead anyway.

"If we can't live together, we'll die together," I told her. That's what I had sworn to myself on the train.

Then I had an idea. Why had they sent my mother to the left, to death? She wasn't even forty. She was in reasonable health. It was that shapeless black dress that made her look old.

"Switch clothes with me," I said. She didn't understand. I couldn't explain. I just had to do it. "Switch clothes with me." Quickly, I took off my red skirt and blue blouse. I made her take off her black dress and put on my clothes. I put on the black dress. I stepped back and looked at her again. She already looked ten years younger, but her cheeks were still pale and sunken. I moistened my finger and rubbed the yellow star on my dress, then rubbed some of the color onto her cheeks. Again and again I daubed her cheeks with color. Perhaps it was just the touch of my finger, not the color of the patch. Her cheeks flushed just a bit.

"Let's go." I didn't wait for her to ask where. I didn't explain my plan. I just pulled her by the hand.

To tell the truth, I didn't exactly have a plan. I just knew that somehow I was going to get us back across that fence to the other side of the camp, away from the dead, to those who still had some hope of living. What did we have to lose? How much more could we suffer?

I led my mother by the hand to the edge of the barracks, so I could peek out and see what was happening. The selection process was continuing. New victims kept arriving from the changing room. A long line of women was bunched together and slowly passing by the tall, handsome doctor. He selected them and sent them whichever way he chose, with small gestures of his hands. Then the Kapos and guards shoved the women to their fate. The guards watched the women who had been chosen for work very closely, making sure they stood in orderly lines of six, but they paid less attention to the women on the other side of the fence who had been selected for death. Their backs were to us, as if we were dead already.

From time to time a large group of women was shoved through the gate toward the death barracks, causing a commotion. I moved forward with my mother, standing with other women so as to be inconspicuous. We got as close as we could to the barbed wire fence, and I waited until another large group of women was about to be pushed through to our side. I saw there was a way of rushing through the opening and melting into the throng of women who hadn't gone through the selection process, simply because the Nazis probably thought no one would ever want to go through twice. A woman on the line, who noticed what I had done for my mother, called me a "wonderchild." That gave me just a tiny bit more faith that my plan would work.

Now a large group of women was bunched at the gate. I moved up, pulling my mother along.

"Where are you taking me?" she asked, nearly weeping.

"To the other side."

"No, leave me here, let me stay here and die. You go by yourself." She began to pull away from me, but I held her hand and wouldn't let her go. I kept my eye on what was happening at the selection point. The guards were about to shove a big group of women through to our side.

"You have to come with me. Now!"

I pulled my mother up to the gate, and during the confusion as the women selected for death were herded through, my mother and I managed to slip back to the other side and join the line of women who hadn't been selected yet. Once we stood among them there was no way of distinguishing us from the rest. We hadn't escaped from anything, really. There was no point in hunting us down.

Now we approached the doctor again. Our hearts beat in anxiety, like everyone else's. Would he send us both to the right, to life, this time? Would he recognize us and have us shot on the spot? Perhaps he would merely punish us by sending us both to the left. His eyes were so sharp. He looked at us so carefully. Did he recognize us? Did he know what we were trying to do?

It is dreadful to have your fate depend on a single person's whim. But this had happened to me time and time again since my earliest childhood.

On Sundays in Frankfurt, when the maid and governess had the day off, we were on our own. Whenever the weather was fine, Father would drive us out of town in our glistening, black Mercedes to the Taunus, a scenic, hilly spot famous as a recreation area. Every weekend, the prosperous householders of Frankfurt used to patronize the fine restaurants there. But it was our custom to go there for Sunday picnics. Father would park the car at a spot with soft grass and shady trees. Then we would bring the wicker basket of kosher food and drink from the car. Mother would spread white linen tablecloths on the grass, and we would sit down. Everything was tidy and impeccable. We ate from high quality paper plates that my father manufactured. Mother would wear a sport dress and flat shoes; Father, a summer suit with a gray English fedora. Picnic or no picnic, we children were expected to keep clean and eat with proper table manners.

One Sunday, to indulge me, Father asked, "Trudi, which way would you like to drive back?" I asked him to take the long, scenic road, and he followed my directions. Soon after we had gone past some of my favorite farmhouses, with sleek, well-tended cows grazing in the meadows, a truck full of soldiers stopped the car and forced us out at gunpoint. This must have been shortly after the Nazis came to power, when I was six.

My brother and I clung to Mother's skirt, listening to the arrogant soldiers as they interrogated my father and humiliated him. My father was no longer a prominent, respected industrialist, a cultured, well-spoken citizen of Frankfurt. Now he was just a filthy Jew. Any lout in the army could beat him or even kill him if he felt like it. One of them screamed, "Kill those filthy Jews immediately! That's an order!" They pointed their guns at us. I was sure they were going to shoot.

The explosions of their bullets already rang in my ears. I cried and hugged my mother. Father stepped forward to stand between the soldiers and his family, as if his body could shield us from their guns. We were trembling with fear, and the soldiers enjoyed the spectacle of our fright, "Listen to the filthy Jews whimper."

At last, one of the soldiers said, "*Ach*, let them go." Maybe he was a sergeant, I don't remember, but I can still imitate just the way he said it: not mercifully, but with contempt, as if we weren't worth wasting bullets on. The soldiers climbed back into their truck and drove off, laughing merrily. I can never forget that moment. The relief at being spared did nothing to erase the horror at being threatened. My life was never the same after that.

We never had another picnic in the Taunus. The secure world of my childhood had been violently overturned. And that was just the first of many times when all that stood between me and certain death was a soldier's caprice. Even now, whenever I am riding in a car, if someone asks me which route to take I cannot answer. I am paralyzed. That innocent question fills me with dread. Suddenly I am a little girl again, and if I give the wrong answer, Nazi stormtroopers will be waiting around the bend. This is not the memory of fear. This is fear itself, ever present, of hideous danger, waiting for me to take a wrong turn.

Such a brush with death would be enough to mark a person for the rest of his life, but it was only the first of many. Once we were shut in the ghetto, not a day passed without equal or greater peril. Any German soldier passing in the street could decide to kill a Jew if he felt like it, and they often did feel like it. They had a daily quota of arbitrary murders. There were frequent selections, inspections, searches, counts—whatever they felt like doing. I learned to smile pleasantly at the soldiers who might kill me, hoping to make them like me just enough to spare me. Up to now, it had worked.

Our unofficial second turn came all too soon. The doctor examined me intently. I smiled up at him, looking into his eyes to see whether he recognized me. His gaze gave away nothing. He did not acknowledge that he might have seen us before. We were not people for him, anyway.

Again I was sent to the right, and this time my mother

was sent after me, to the lines of women waiting to be sent to labor camps. I had succeeded. My mother was with me again. We stood close to each other, trembling in a line of six women, part of a labor brigade now, not sentenced to immediate death.

But don't think we were full of joy. We were full of fear.

From the Freezer to the Bridge

CHAPTER TWO

When I look back on my youth, I see that at every step of the way I lost something. By the time I reached the concentration camp in Stutthof, I had been brought almost to utter deprivation. I often think of everything that was snatched away from me—my home, my father, my grandparents and uncles and aunts, my native language and culture. I think about these things so that I can recover some of this lost world, at least in memory, so it will live on.

When I was six, my family was driven into exile from Frankfurt to Memel. Nevertheless, my parents made sure that my childhood was happy and fairly secure, even after the Russians invaded Lithuania in 1939. But my childhood came to a gloomy end in a meat freezer, among skinned animal carcasses hanging on sharp hooks.

Naturally, the shocking incident after our Sunday picnic in the scenic Taunus, when the German soldiers nearly shot us just for being Jews, had cast a heavy cloud over the security of my childhood. I was too young to express it in words, but I knew that the rules of the world had changed profoundly. Before that, I had believed what I had been taught, that God would protect you from harm if you were good. Afterward I knew that even good, innocent people could be shot in cold blood if a common soldier felt like shooting them.

My early childhood in Frankfurt, Germany, had been

privileged and protected. My father, Philip Simon, had been its guarantor. When I was little, I thought of myself as Father's girl. He was a formal, Orthodox German Jew of the old school. His father had been a rabbi in Memel, the Baltic port that was to be our first place of refuge. As a child, my father had been taught what was right and wrong, and he never questioned what he had been taught. He did his best to pass his beliefs on to his own children by providing us with a model of correct behavior.

Father was at least ten years older than Mother. He was a refined, formal person. He always wore a business suit with a bow tie, and he smoked a pipe. He was short and slightly stocky, with a dignified presence. He was husband and provider, and he always did his best to spare my mother any worry or difficulty. He took his responsibilities so seriously that I remember feeling sorry for him, because the burden of supporting us fell upon his shoulders alone. With old-fashioned confidence in his values, Father set the tone for our family. He was a strict man, but I remember his strictness with great love. If only we, his children, had been able to grow up in the kind of world he wanted to make for us! But history wrenched his world apart, and nothing could have prepared him or us for what we were to face.

Father carried himself with assurance. In Frankfurt he was a successful manufacturer, and he willingly embraced the social responsibilities that went with affluence in our society: charity, support for Jewish institutions, personal honor, and high ethical standards. Although he was not born in Frankfurt, he was a respected member of that deeply rooted community, where Jews had been living without interruption since at least the fourteenth century. They rightly considered themselves part of the landscape.

My father and his brother owned a paper factory. We lived in a spacious apartment near the zoo. Life was very comfortable for us. Mother had a maid and a cook, and we children had a nanny named Candy, a Gentile woman, to take care of us. She used to speak to Manfred and me in English. That was part of the proper European education we were meant to receive.

Along with her other talents and abilities, Candy was a registered nurse. Her starched uniform and the nurse's cap with a red Star of David on it left a deep impression on me. Once my brother and I caught scarlet fever, a dangerous, often fatal disease at the time. Instead of sending us to the hospital, my parents had us quarantined in our room for weeks, and Candy was the only one who went back and forth between us and the outside world. My parents had a window specially installed in the door, and I remember them looking in at us through the glass panes.

The first years of my life were violently severed from the rest. I was born into a secure world, with solid hopes for the future. That was all stolen from me. I look back at my childhood in Frankfurt with great longing. Manfred and I were among the best-dressed children in the city. My mother had elegant clothes made for us, the kind you see in formal photographs of the time. But not even a snapshot remains from our childhood in Frankfurt.

Right now, if you were to ask me when things took place, I wouldn't want to remember those days with dates, names, and addresses. I prefer just to remember the atmosphere of love, comfort, and security. But we had to leave everyone and everything behind, simply because we were Jewish. I keep telling myself we never committed any crime, we weren't bad people, there was no reason to punish us for anything. When you have lost so much and suffered so much, you can begin to feel guilty, as if you had done something to deserve all that suffering. But we weren't guilty of anything. I keep reminding myself of that truth.

Unlike most German Jews, Father had no illusions about the possibility of living in security under Hitler—perhaps because of that terrifying incident on the way home from the picnic—and he was willing to take his chances as a refugee. The semiautonomous port city of Memel on the Baltic coast was a logical choice to flee to, for personal as well as political reasons. Both my parents had been born in Memel while it was still part of the German Empire, and my mother's parents had remained there. Every summer our family used to vacation in Memel, so after the summer of 1933, my mother and we children simply stayed on.

Candy didn't come to Memel with us. We brought very few of our belongings: some furniture, some silver, a few paintings. I took along my beloved teddy bears and Leslie, my doll.

It wasn't such a simple matter for Father to join us. He tried to remove whatever cash he could from Germany—illegally, of course—by sneaking across the border into Holland, and then he entered Memel as a stateless refugee. He had no rights of citizenship in his native city because it had passed from the German Empire after World War I. All during the years we lived in Memel, Father had to keep renewing his visa. I can't remember what our own status was. That was of no concern to a little girl.

We lived with my mother's parents until Father managed to join us within a few months. Then we moved to our own apartment, far more modest than the one we had left in Frankfurt, but pleasant. Father set himself up in business again, this time as a manufacturer's representative for Dutch building materials firms.

Although Memel is known today as Klaipeda and belongs to Lithuania, it had been a German city since its founding in the Middle Ages. After World War I it became a bone of contention between Lithuania, which had no other port, and Poland. Although it was more or less taken over by Lithuania, most of the population still spoke German, and I attended a German school. Classes were held on Saturday, but Father intervened to have me excused from tests and homework on Saturdays, so I wouldn't have to write on the Sabbath.

I can't remember any anti-Semitic incidents at school, even though there were few Jewish pupils. The teachers were fair, and I was popular. I especially liked to appear in class plays, and I dreamed of becoming an actress.

In Memel, I remained close to my father. He used to take me to synagogue with him. The memory of the melodies they sang there lives with me to this day, especially the beautiful tune for Kol Nidre, the Yom Kippur hymn. In Frankfurt Father had attended the large, official, Orthodox synagogue of the community, and in Memel we attended a similar kind of synagogue. I learned some prayers and Bible stories, but I didn't go to religious school in the afternoons. Only boys were sent.

I like to think of my father as a *tzaddik*, a righteous Jew, but a true *tzaddik* is a poor man who gives away everything, and Father was not poor until we were confined in the ghetto. He always provided well for us. But he was more charitable than my mother thought we could afford to be. I remember going shopping with him for food to send to suffering Jews in Poland. We went to the best kosher delicatessens in Memel (and later in Kovno). He chose the highest quality goods in the store, better food than we ate ourselves. He insisted that you had to give the best to the poor. That was his understanding of the religious duty of charity. In my own work today, providing free dental care for people on welfare in Jerusalem, I follow exactly the same principle.

Even as a refugee in a world that had begun to collapse, my father maintained his demanding standards. We children were expected to behave properly. Manfred and I were infallibly polite and respectful with our parents. We had to be. One Saturday morning, as I was walking to synagogue with my father, I saw the word *"Hure"* (whore) carved on a wall. I'm sure I didn't know what it meant; otherwise I wouldn't have dared to utter it in front of my father. But for some reason, innocently, I did read it out loud. Punishment was swift and immediate: three days of "house arrest." I could only wave sadly to my best friend, Bessie, from the third-story window of my bedroom, where I was confined. She sent messages to me, telling me what homework I had to do. At the time I thought this would be one of my bitterest childhood memories.

Mother wasn't strictly Orthodox in her outlook. She

was traditional and went along with my father. But she never wore a wig like an ultra-Orthodox woman, and she seldom went to synagogue with us, except on the High Holidays.

One thing she shared with my father was her concern for the poor. In Frankfurt she helped to found a kindergarten for the Jewish poor. That was in 1931. But she didn't go as far in her charity as Father did. Mother thought that family came before everything.

She played piano well. She had graduated from the music academy in Frankfurt, and she used to give piano lessons. In Frankfurt, I think she did it mainly to keep busy, but in Memel it was for the income, too. We always had a piano in the house, even after we fled Memel for Kovno.

I took piano lessons, but not with my mother. I remember playing "*Für Elise*," and I used to play duets with her. I was making good progress until the war interrupted my studies.

My close connection with Mother developed in Memel. Perhaps she had been somewhat distant from us children while we lived in Frankfurt, because she had the nanny to take care of us. She was a bright woman, with a well developed intelligence. She read widely, and she had a good sense of judgment: she was wise. Even as a child, I could talk with her about everything. She was also a modern person.

I have very fond memories of Memel. All during the time our family lived there, I used to visit my mother's parents frequently. We spoke politely and formally with our grandparents. We didn't use Yiddish nicknames like

"Bubbie" and "Zaydie." We called them "Grossmutter" and "Grossvater." We always spoke German with them, never Yiddish, which we didn't know. All the Jews of Memel spoke German.

My mother's parents lived in a pleasant, middle-class house, and Grossmutter used to give me cookies and treats, just like everybody's grandmother. I used to sit on Grossvater's lap and twirl his blond curls with my fingers. I always hoped that when I had a son, he would have blond curls like grandpa's. That wish came true.

I also got to know other members of my mother's family in Memel. Mother was the oldest of four. Her two brothers, Benno and Jakob, were both serious young professionals beginning their careers. Benno was a lawyer and Jakob a doctor; neither was married. I was particularly close to my mother's youngest sister, my aunt Tita, who was in her late teens. I was Tita's pet. She was the one who used to dress me up and take me to the cafés in Memel, where they held five o'clock dances for children. The band played and there were waltz and tango contests. The winning children got balloons as prizes. I was just eight or nine at the time and small for my age, but I loved to perform in front of audiences. My dresses were always cute, and I never sat out a dance. I often came home tingling with pleasure, grasping a bunch of brightly colored balloons.

Tita married a Jew from Riga, and they were both killed by the Nazis. Recently, one of my few surviving cousins sent me a photograph taken in Memel in the late 1930s at my aunt Tita's wedding. That is the only family picture remaining from my entire childhood. In fact, it is the only physical object in my possession that links me to my life before the war. I have no other souvenir from that time.

In the picture I'm standing in the back row on a chair next to my uncle Benno. In the Slobodka ghetto the Nazis murdered Benno before his mother's eyes. But I'm getting ahead of myself. You can't see any of that in the picture, where we're all happy for Aunt Tita. She and the groom are sitting at the head of the table, looking serious. Jakob, her older brother, is sitting at her side, and next to him are her parents, my maternal grandparents, looking proud. My mother is standing just behind her mother and, on the other side of the table, at the left edge of the picture, stands my father, looking very dapper with a black tie over his starched shirtfront, a white handkerchief in his breast pocket, and a black satin yarmulke on his head. He is a kind, intelligent, dignified man, with a clear gaze.

My brother, Manfred, isn't in the picture. He was probably away at the Jewish boarding school in Sweden where my father sent him to continue the rigorous education he had begun in Frankfurt. He had just completed his studies when the war began. My father sent for him so the family would be together, a decision that could have cost my brother his life, but at the time there was no way of knowing what was the right thing to do.

I don't remember Memel as a particularly pretty city, just a port. My grandparents had a summer house in a resort area called Polangen. To get there you had to take the steamer that continued on to Koenigsberg. Polangen was my favorite place. I had many friends who also went there every summer vacation.

We stayed in Memel until the Germans took it over on March 21, 1939. At that time we left for Kovno, Lithuania, with my mother's parents and the rest of her family. We didn't flee in abject poverty as refugees. We were able to take many of our belongings. I still had my teddy bears and Leslie. Father continued to represent Dutch firms in Lithuania.

Kovno was a much more sophisticated city than Memel, with a lot more charm. We moved into an apartment on a fine residential street, Kestiucho Street. The Hebrew Realgymnasia, the school I attended, was at the other end of that broad avenue, and the opera house stood across from it. Our apartment was on the fourth floor, and Lena, a Lithuanian housemaid, came every day to clean and cook.

I wasn't frightened by the international situation. What upset me was the change in schools. I was switched from a German school to a Jewish school where the language of instruction was Hebrew, which I did not know. Suddenly I was thrown in with new children in a strange city, and I had to catch up and fit in. I hated being an outsider, behind in all my studies because of the language.

I worked as hard as I could and was making good progress, but within a short time I had to make another difficult adjustment in school. The Soviets took over Kovno in June 1940, and suddenly it was forbidden to teach Hebrew. Yiddish became the language of instruction. It was enough like German that I didn't have a lot of trouble learning it, and to this day I know Yiddish well. They also taught Russian and Lithuanian in school, and I didn't know those languages at all. Always hard-working and anxious to do well, I had tutors who helped me memorize poems in Russian and Lithuanian, and I was soon among the better pupils in my class. Despite the difficulty, I loved learning the new languages. If anyone asked me what I wanted to be when I grew up, I would say, "A translator or an actress," and whenever the teacher asked for volunteers to appear in a school play, my hand was the first one up. But I didn't get a chance to make any real close friends in my new school. I must have been confused and disoriented by the changes. I remember those first two years in Kovno as lonely ones.

One of my greatest sources of pleasure while I lived in Kovno was ice skating (*zhozhikla* in Lithuanian). There were two skating rinks I used to frequent. One was on the way to school, and I skated there twice a week. The other was across town, and I went there less often. I loved to dress up in my skating costume and practice figure eights and other tricks. To this day, when I get to a city with a public skating rink, if there's time I rent skates and recapture my childhood, *zhozhikla*!

The Kovno opera house with its cupola was my second source of pleasure. It was as beautiful an opera house as I've ever seen since. My parents often took me to hear the great Kipras Petrauskas. No performance I hear today can rival the magic of his voice, the rapture of hearing great music at an impressionable age.

We lived pretty much undisturbed after the Soviets took over Kovno. My main memory is of the Russian women, whose clothes seemed funny and rustic to me. Sometimes they wore what looked like nightgowns. Food was rationed, but the Russian regime wasn't particularly oppressive, as far as I remember. And we children weren't frightened by the war, which seemed far away.

Then in June 1941 our lives changed completely. We heard that the Soviets had decided to deport all the bourgeois Jewish families to Siberia, and we knew we were on the list. The word "Siberia" conjured up immense horrors in my mind. Even in my father's more balanced opinion, no fate could possibly be worse than Siberia. We had heard plenty of rumors about the inhuman conditions in the labor camps there. Father didn't think my mother could possibly withstand the arctic winters because of her heart condition, which had resulted from a childhood illness. And how could he, a refined man in his late forties who had never done hard physical labor in his life, become a lumberjack? Certainly Manfred and I, two coddled Jewish children, could never survive in the rough-and-tumble world of that isolated frontier. The only thing to do was to flee. Everything was arranged for us to run away to Shanghai, but events moved too fast. Our forced departure for Siberia was imminent.

We had a summer house in a resort town at the seashore, so we sped there in the family car. It was a tense ride. My parents discussed their plans softly, and we children listened. Father intended to lay low until the Russians finished the deportations to Siberia. Then we could leave for Shanghai, as planned.

Father parked the car in a back street and left us for a moment. I could hear a band playing a Beethoven overture in the park. Soon Father returned with a man I did not recognize. They spoke warmly to each other, like good friends. Later Father told us he was Jonas, the butcher.

Our summer house was near Jonas's shop, and Father had somehow made his acquaintance. He certainly had never bought meat from Jonas, because my family was strictly Orthodox and ate only kosher meat. Perhaps they had met while strolling on the beach. Father must have sensed that Jonas was someone he could count on in a pinch, though Jonas didn't hide us solely out of the goodness of his heart.

I remember seeing the money change hands. Then Jonas led us furtively around the back to the delivery entrance of his shop. We slipped down the steps into his basement meat freezer.

We wrapped ourselves in our warmest winter coats and blankets and sat down to wait in hiding until the danger was past—perhaps overnight, we thought.

The time dragged on, but Jonas didn't come to tell us the coast was clear. There was no longer any difference between day and night. Time, too, was frozen. Every minute seemed to last forever. How long would we be in that dark, damp, frigid cellar? I was just a girl. I kept asking my parents, "What time is it? How much longer do we have to stay here?" They couldn't answer me because they didn't know. Suspense made every minute seem an hour.

I was just a girl. Did I understand the gravity of our situation? I think so, as much as someone so young can understand something beyond any experience she or her parents have ever had. More than anything else, I understood the anxious expressions on my parents' faces. They tried to be calm and cheerful, but how long can you keep up a false front? Hiding was a gamble that might not pay off. One full day passed, but it was still not safe to leave. Our patience was almost gone. We might sit in the freezer for a week and still walk right out into the arms of the Soviet police. Yet Father spoke softly to us, calming us down and giving us hope.

———

Three times a day Jonas came downstairs with hot food and whatever news he had, which wasn't very much. In the outside world the situation was fluid, and it was hard to get reliable information. Even though we were wrapped in blankets up to our eyes, we were freezing. We needed the hot meals and ate them with relish, even though the food wasn't kosher. I had never eaten nonkosher food before. I knew it must be a real emergency if we were ignoring such an important principle in our lives. It was terribly dreary and gloomy in the freezer, and we had to be absolutely quiet while the shop was open. No one except Jonas—not even his wife and children—knew we were there. Jonas's life was at risk as well. If we had been discovered, he would have been shot or sent to Siberia with us.

I had been frightened for my life once before, when the soldiers stopped us on our way home from the picnic in the Taunus, but I had never been frightened for such a long time. The cold seeped into us and made us shiver, but whenever we heard footsteps approaching the door, a strong hand opening the latch, we trembled more violently. Was it Jonas, bringing us food and news? Or was it Russian soldiers coming to shoot us or drag us away to Siberia?

I was aching with questions, questions that have been turning over and over in my mind for nearly fifty years. Why did we have to hide? Why did the Russians want to send us to Siberia? What had we done wrong? I didn't dare ask my parents all these questions then. They were in no mood to grope for impossible answers. Nobody could find an answer then, nor can one be found today.

I remember staring and staring at the skinned carcasses of quartered cows, lambs, and pigs, and having nightmares that they would attack us. The smell of aging meat filled my nostrils. To this day, whenever I see meat displayed in a butcher shop, I shiver. I visualize human bodies hanging naked on those cruel hooks: my family's bodies. Soon we would turn into frozen meat ourselves. I wanted to ask my father, "How much worse could it be in Siberia?"

We hid in that freezer for three days, until we were stiff with cold, even though we made sure to get up and walk around often enough to keep our blood flowing. During the whole time there wasn't a moment when I wasn't terrified. Despite our warm clothes and blankets, we felt numb and half-dead, inside and out, like those awful animal carcasses. On the third day, after the deportations to Siberia were over, Jonas told us we could go in safety. We stumbled up his cellar stairs into a bright summer day. The street didn't look real. We blinked and shielded our eyes from the sun. Wrapped in our heavy winter clothes, we still shivered. We had to take off our coats to warm up. It seemed like hours before the sun soaked out the accumulated chill of that freezer.

We no longer felt totally vulnerable. We were just a pale, bleary family dressed in good but rumpled clothes. We got in our car and drove back to Kovno, and Father resumed preparations for flight to Shanghai. But Germany attacked Russia on June 22, 1941, and soon the Jews who stayed behind in Kovno had reason to wish they had been sent to Siberia. The Shanghai option was dead. No one was going anywhere.

For me, the Holocaust began in Jonas's meat freezer. That was the end of any semblance of normal life for us as a Jewish family. We had been driven from our home twice, first from Frankfurt, then from Memel. Who could tell how long we would be able to stay in our apartment in Kovno? We knew we couldn't count on Gentiles any longer. Jonas was an exception, and even he had to be paid well for his kindness. We also knew we wouldn't give up. We would do everything we could to survive together as a family.

━━━━━

During the German invasion, after the Russians had fled, Lithuanian partisans went on a rampage. Before the Nazis clamped the iron vise of their fierce order down on the population, there was a period of terror and anarchy. People had scores to settle, real and imagined, for things that had happened under the Russians. Lithuanians who had been our neighbors, our customers, and our partners in business took up the profitable sport of shooting Jews. It was like that scene from my childhood in Frankfurt all over again, only much, much worse.

I still can't understand how people who had lived in peace as neighbors, customers, and partners of the Jews for generations suddenly became murderers. It changes the way you look at people. You see some young men in the street, and you wonder, "Could they start shooting people at random, too?" Groups of uniformed thugs roamed the streets, killing and looting. We heard them going from house to house, breaking in, lining up Jews, and slaughtering them, family by family. Peeping from our windows, we could see them carrying off whatever they could steal.

I found myself longing for the safe concealment of Jonas's freezing cellar. We huddled in our living room, sitting in silence, praying that the marauders would pass over our fourth-floor apartment. Then we heard them stomping up the stairs. It was only a short time before they reached us. They easily battered down the locked door and stormed in.

There was nowhere to hide, so we didn't even try. Six or seven hulking young men in uniforms, Lithuanians carrying guns, filled the room with furious danger. We were trapped, helpless in our own living room. It was unbelievable that these barbarians were in my mother's sanctuary. She had worked so hard to decorate it, to make it a civilized place, to keep it clean and tidy. How could their filthy boots trample and sully our carpets!

"Face the wall, you Jewish pigs!"

The image of the skinned pig carcasses hanging in Jonas's freezer flashed before my eyes. Suddenly I felt ice cold again. Manfred and I squeezed as close to our parents as possible.

Then, astonishingly, Lena, our slender Lithuanian maid, spoke up for us. She had worked for us ever since we had arrived in Kovno. I loved Lena. She helped me learn Lithuanian. Lena was petite and pretty and wore a black uniform with a white apron. She pleaded with the invaders: "Have pity on this good family. Can't you see they're fine, cultured people? Don't you have any respect?"

How would the killers react? With our faces to the wall, we could only guess what was happening. Perhaps they would kill Lena for standing up for us. Soon shots would be fired in that special room where our family had eaten meals, celebrated holidays, listened to music—and that would be the end of everything. The wallpaper before my eyes would be the last thing I ever saw. Our bloody bodies would be left in a heap, and the looters would ransack our apartment.

A miracle happened. Our maid's words swayed the killers. They lowered their rifles and left us in peace. They grabbed a few valuables and smashed some knickknacks on their way out, but at least we were all still alive. We hugged Lena and clung together in silent gratitude, but we cringed as we heard shots fired in our neighbors' apartments. The other Jews didn't have a Lena to intercede on their behalf.

When they took over, the Nazis put an end to random looting and shooting by the Lithuanians—and replaced it with much more systematic and brutal slaughter.

The German attack on Russia began on June 22, 1941. By July 10, the Nazis had taken firm enough control to issue an order that Jews were to wear yellow Jewish stars as of July 12. I can't remember exactly how they distributed the stars. I think my mother sewed them on our clothes, front and back. I never felt ashamed of wearing the Jewish star. The Nazis never made me feel that being Jewish was a sin.

After that time of random terror, we were almost relieved when the Germans imposed some kind of order. But events moved very fast. If we Jews had any illusions about the treatment we could expect from the Germans, they were short-lived.

How can one communicate the strange and cruel feeling of dislocation that afflicted me? German was my native language. In my family we prided ourselves on speaking it well. The children's books I loved were all in German. My friends and teachers in school in Memel had been Germans. But now Germans had become killers. Nothing they said or did could be trusted. Everything was merely a mask for murder.

In July and August the Germans hounded the thirty thousand Jews remaining in Kovno across the Nemunas River to the suburb of Slobodka, where they established a ghetto. It took days to concentrate us all in the ghetto. That was the absolute end of our "comfortable" life. Now, with all the tens of thousands of other Jews from Kovno, driven from our homes, we were reduced to only those possessions that we could carry ourselves. I took some of my pretty dresses and a few trinkets, which I thought of as valuable jewelry. I wasn't a babyish little girl, but still I took my teddy bear and Leslie, my doll. I had brought Leslie with me from Frankfurt and cherished her in Memel. She was the last vestige of my happy childhood, and I managed to keep her until the destruction of the ghetto in 1944.

Those who could afford it hired wagons from the Lithuanians at exorbitant prices. Our family managed to get a wagon. We piled in it everything we could save and pulled it through the streets in the hot sun. The poor people had to carry all their belongings in their arms. Children who could barely walk themselves dragged along whatever they could. Cruel German soldiers shouted and rushed us on. The sun beat down on us. We were sweating, panting under our burdens, terrified. We all crossed the river on a broad concrete bridge, sick and healthy, old and young, petrified mothers holding babies in their arms. I kept thinking about the Exodus from Egypt, thousands of Jews swarming across the Red Sea with all their earthly goods on their backs. But we were not passing from slavery to freedom. We were entering bondage far more cruel than anything the Egyptians had inflicted on the Israelites.

Once we were in the ghetto area there was another bridge to cross, a narrow, wooden bridge that the Nazis had forced the Jews to build. I had always thought of bridges as symbols of hope, structures connecting places, bringing people over an obstacle. But this was a bridge of despair.

Here and there the walls of Slobodka were splotched with patches of bright red, and that cheered me up because red was my favorite color. I remember trying to cheer up my dejected parents, saying, "Look at the pretty paint." They didn't have the heart to tell me it was human blood.

Exile
to
the Ghetto

CHAPTER THREE

My childhood ended on August 15, 1941, when the Nazis enclosed the entire ghetto of Kovno behind a wire fence. German soldiers were on guard all the time as we moved into the ghetto, shouting threats over loudspeakers to force us to move faster. No one dared open his mouth to complain or protest, even to ask a simple question. At any moment we could be shot. To this day, whenever I hear a loudspeaker in the street, I'm frightened.

We became prisoners, forbidden to leave the ghetto, crowded together in housing inadequate for our numbers, cut off from the outside world, deprived of contact with other Jewish communities, and utterly without protection. There was no impartial court of law or independent government to which we could appeal. We had no political power whatsoever, and no access to what one would call "the media" today. We were surrounded by German troops and by a Lithuanian population that had proven itself to be murderously hostile to Jews.

As a child I was not aware of the broad picture. I only knew that life had become extremely dangerous for Jews, and that I was no longer free to come and go—which was very painful.

The Slobodka neighborhood, which the Nazis turned into the ghetto, had been a powerful center of Orthodox Jewish learning, the home of many important yeshivas, including the eminent Slobodka Yeshiva and one of the greatest institutions of learning in the Jewish world, the center of a powerful moral and intellectual tradition. This yeshiva had been the focus of an intense ultra-Orthodox community: teachers, rabbis, and other very religious people who wished to live in an atmosphere of holiness.

In late June, before the Germans crowded us into Slobodka, they permitted the Lithuanians to commit a savage massacre there, desecrating synagogues and Torah scrolls and slaughtering more than a thousand people, mostly rabbis, yeshiva students, and their families. It was their blood that had reddened the walls of the town.

After the Orthodox community of Slobodka was slaughtered, there still wasn't room for all the rest of the Jews in Kovno. The Gentiles of Slobodka, who had lived in poor public housing, were ordered to move out, and Jews took their place, trading fine, roomy apartments in desirable neighborhoods for one-room dwellings in workers' tenements.

My family ended up in a single room which measured about ten by twelve feet, with nothing in it but four beds and a closet. Outside in the corridor was a small kitchen and bathroom. Except for our three days in the freezer, we had never lived in such cramped quarters. Nevertheless I remember being glad when we finally got there. We had been driven from our home and herded through the streets, not knowing what was in store for us or whether we would survive to see the sunset that day. Now at least we had someplace to live. It was a small room, but it had four walls and a roof, and it was ours.

When the Germans ordered us to leave our homes in

Kovno and move to the ghetto in Slobodka, they told us to bring along all our money and valuables. Trying to guess what the future had in store for us, my parents took this as a good sign. They reasoned that the Germans must be planning some kind of a new life for us—not one as good as our life before the Russians invaded Lithuania and not even one as good as the short period before we were sent to the ghetto, when we had to wear yellow stars and face all kinds of arbitrary discrimination, but still a life. If they planned to kill us, why would they have us bring our valuables?

I remember packing before the move. Our household was already reduced compared to what it had been in Frankfurt and Memel, but we still had fine, lovely things: furniture, carpets, and bric-a-brac that we would have to leave behind, and clothes that were too bulky or too fancy to pack—my mother's most elegant dresses, my father's well-tailored suits, my own party dresses and patent leather shoes. It was painful to say goodbye to some of the dolls and books I couldn't fit into my suitcase, and to the pretty skirts and blouses I would never wear again.

My mother took all her jewelry, not a huge treasure but things that were precious to her because they had been presents from my father, given on special occasions during the years of their marriage: a few gold rings and bracelets, a necklace or two with precious stones, a pair of pearl earrings. She went through them one by one, placing them carefully in her jewel box. My father added things of his own: a gold watch and chain, some tie pins, cuff links, studs, and a couple of rings.

They realized they would probably have to trade all

these objects for food in the uncertain future. How many loaves of bread would Mother's engagement ring fetch? How many eggs was this cameo brooch worth? At least the jewels offered our family some hope for security.

We unloaded the little wagon and arranged our things as best we could. Exhausted, my parents rested, but Manfred and I were restless. The room smelled somewhat like Jonas's butcher shop. Somebody had apparently thrown buckets of red paint on the walls inside as well. I went over and put my finger on a patch of red. No one had to explain anything to me. I realized it was human blood.

Our room was in a large block of tenements, long buildings with separate entrances arranged around a big courtyard. The buildings were three stories tall, long structures like trains. My mother's parents and my two uncles settled in a nearby apartment.

If you can talk about good fortune in such circumstances, our family had the good fortune of remaining together. When we were driven from Memel to Kovno by the Nazis, my mother's family had come with us, except for my aunt Tita, who moved to Riga with her husband. My two uncles, Jakob and Benno, were very devoted to their parents and lived at home with them. In the ghetto my grandparents and my two uncles lived nearby, and it was still pleasant to visit my grandparents, a reminder of old times. We brought food to my grandparents, who weren't entitled to rations because they didn't work. I used to steal food for them when I worked outside the ghetto.

When Father saw how small and bare our room was, he realized there was no safe place to hide the jewels. What was to stop anyone from sneaking into the house while we were out and stealing our things? We couldn't keep someone at home to guard the room twenty-four hours a day.

Behind our building there was a large untended courtyard. One dark night, soon after our arrival in the ghetto, Father and Manfred went out secretly and buried most of the jewels behind the house. "Now we have money in the bank," Father joked when they came back inside and rinsed the earth from their hands.

Neglected courtyards lay behind all the tenements. The younger children played wild games among the weeds, far from their parents' eyes. But I didn't want to join them. A quick change had taken place in my personality. I realized this was no time for play. For me, those neglected plots of land were a symbol of danger, not of freedom.

I don't remember having friends my own age in the ghetto. I had only been living in Lithuania for two years before the war, not enough time to make really close friends. I wasn't a lonely little girl, but I was independent.

The Nazis organized the Judenrat right away, an administrative committee composed of Jewish functionaries who were forced to execute the Nazis' orders. Father began working as a clerk in an office there, with about eight other men.

A few days after the ghetto was closed off, an announcement was made over loudspeakers: Special work was to be given to university students and graduates. There were only a few hundred such jobs, so everyone who was interested should report immediately to a certain square.

Many of the Jews of Kovno were well-educated professionals, engineers, physicians, pharmacists. They encouraged their children to study and get ahead. The war had halted their progress, but now the Nazis seemed to be offering a special chance to these young men. Their education would pay off.

Hundreds of bright young men reported to the square with their diplomas and matriculation certificates, looking forward to beginning work so they could support their parents and make it through the war. The Germans took them away, and nothing was heard of them for a couple of days. We later learned that every one of them was mowed down in cold blood with machine guns.

——

Life in the ghetto was a dull, depressing grind, punctuated by violent tragedies. Our daily routine included constant random murders, lineups, selections, and what the Germans called *Aktionen*. They systematically liquidated those who couldn't work, but you weren't safe even if you were fit to work, because there were arbitrary murders as well. They took great pleasure in killing us. They had a daily kill quota: a certain number of Jews were shot at random every day. The Nazis simply seized people in the street or pulled them out of their houses, for no particular reason.

One Sunday we heard shots from the tenement block near ours. For some reason these particular shots alarmed my mother more than usual, although shots were often fired in the ghetto. We were allowed to leave our homes, but it was dangerous to be out in the streets; German soldiers constantly roamed about, and they killed people whenever they felt like it. You never knew when you or someone you loved might be arrested or shot down.

It was spring. I remember the fresh air, the gentle sun,

the leafy trees. The yards behind the houses were full of high, untended grass and weeds and colorful wildflowers. The shots came from very close to Grandma and Grandpa's house. My mother knew: "It's in my parents' courtyard." She started to rush out of the house, toward the shooting, a foolhardy thing to do. I couldn't stop her, so I followed her.

When we got to my grandparents' courtyard we saw Grandma first. Two soldiers were holding her, and she was straining against their arms, trying to reach the end of the courtyard. Grandma was screaming. I never imagined she could scream so loudly. Then we saw other soldiers dragging Uncle Benno toward a wall. The soldiers had broken into my grandparents' apartment and grabbed Benno. They had kicked and dragged him downstairs. Other soldiers seized Grandma, making her follow them. She was pleading for mercy, which amused them.

Why had they picked Benno as their victim? He was a serious young man, a good son, a sweet uncle. He wasn't involved with the underground, he wasn't a leader. He was a professional, a lawyer. They did it because the Germans wanted to humiliate the Jewish intellectuals, to show us that a Jew's personal qualities and achievements meant nothing to them. Benno had been doing hard labor like everyone else, but that wasn't sufficient degradation. The Nazis decided to include him in their daily quota of murders.

The soldiers had taken only Benno and his mother, leaving Grandpa and Jakob inside. They had been afraid to follow the soldiers downstairs. They would surely have been killed too. My uncle didn't say a word. Hysterical with apprehension and grief, Grandma was forced to watch her own son be slaughtered.

The soldiers holding him knew who he was. The one in charge said, "Now you're going to see your son the lawyer get shot right in front of your eyes. We're going to get rid of him." Grandma begged for mercy: "I nursed him at my breast. You can't take away my son. It's impossible!" But the soldiers enjoyed their work.

They pushed Grandma and Benno out into the garden. They dragged Benno over to the wall while two of them held my grandmother. They shoved him against the wall and shot him in the back three times.

Uncle Benno could have done nothing to escape death. That was the case with most of the people whom the Nazis murdered. But others died because they gave up hope.

I remember mothers in the ghetto who lost all hope of survival for themselves, who accepted death as inevitable, but who couldn't accept the idea that their babies would share their fate. Sometimes they managed to make an arrangement with a Lithuanian peasant family who was willing to take a baby, often for money. I witnessed such scenes in our apartment block. Mothers would wrap up their infants and cushion them in jute bags. Then they would drug them with sleeping powder so they wouldn't cry, and at night they threw the babies over the ghetto fence to the waiting peasants. That memory—of Jewish mothers casting their babies away to Gentile peasants, because that was their children's only hope for life—dwells with me as strongly as anything that happened to me. When I had my own babies, and later, when I became a grandmother, I tried to imagine what was in those young mothers' minds and hearts when they gave up their babies—such tragic, desperate, selfless love.

This was the only chance those babies had for survival. All of them would have been killed in one *Aktion* or another before the ghetto was liquidated. Some of the babies actually did survive. A cousin of mine was thrown over the fence and kept during the war by a peasant. Somehow she was returned to her natural family and came to Israel from the Soviet Union in the early 1970s. Another relative of mine was saved by a Volksdeutsch family who raised him, and he's still in close contact with them.

Everything was scarce in the ghetto, especially food. The Germans issued ration tickets for staples, never enough to feed us properly—a few grams of bread or flour, some root vegetables, no green vegetables or fruit, meat or dairy products. We had to supplement the rations with whatever we could buy on the sly, for exorbitant prices, from the Lithuanian peasants who found ways of making contact with us for profit. So it was reassuring to know we could take out my mother's jewelry and sell it when we ran out of food.

In September 1941 the Germans issued a proclamation: The Jews of the Kovno ghetto were to turn over all their valuables. They were to place them on their kitchen tables, and the Germans would go from apartment to apartment and confiscate them. If anyone was caught hiding gold or jewels after the date of the search, a hundred Jews would be killed.

Another ray of hope was blotted out.

We were frightened and in doubt. Only my brother was confident. Father and he had hidden the jewels where no one could ever find them. "The children have run all over the courtyard and there's no trace of the hole where we left them. Why should we turn anything over?"

Mother objected: "If they come and we have nothing, that will arouse their suspicion. They'll search us, beat us, maybe kill us. We have to sacrifice at least some of the jewels."

Father explained the dilemma clearly. We were damned if we did and damned if we didn't. "If we dig some of the jewels up now and hide the rest, someone might see us and inform on us. No matter how careful we are, we'll leave signs on the earth, and people will notice someone has been digging. If the Nazis notice the hole and find our valuables, they'll drag people out of the nearest house and shoot them. If the Nazis don't notice, some thief will surely see it and dig them up himself."

What could we do? The hour set by the Nazis approached rapidly, and we still hadn't made up our minds. Those few jewels, the last remnant of our family's wealth, our last link with the big house in Frankfurt and my happy childhood there, stood between us and hunger. They were our whole fortune, a modest handful of valuables. Outside the ghetto they wouldn't have been a huge fortune, but here they were everything, and we had to surrender them. It hurt. It was insulting. It was cruel. Most of all, what did it mean for our future?

Everywhere in the ghetto, Jews were agonizing over the same decision: to give up the valuables or to face the constant risk of cruel death. Was it more of a risk, really? No matter what, the Nazis were shooting people in cold blood whenever they felt like it. No one knew when he left the house whether he would come back home that day. Why not take the chance? Eventually the Russians might force the Germans back out of Lithuania. The war might end. Then we could dig up our jewels and have something to start a new life with. If we handed them over, we'd have nothing.

I think in the end my father decided to dig up the jewels and surrender all of them to save innocent lives. If the Nazis ever discovered them, and if children happened to be playing in the courtyard near the hiding place, then the Nazis would simply shoot down the children, or any other innocent bystander. So, an hour before the Germans were to come and collect the valuables, Manfred and my father dug up our jewels again. We arranged them neatly on the kitchen table and looked at them wistfully while we waited for the Germans. So many memories clung to those jewels: Mother's birthdays, my parents' wedding anniversaries, happy occasions celebrated with a precious gift. And those jewels had embodied so much hope for us. They might have been the difference between starvation and survival.

When the soldiers burst into our room, filling it with their dark, threatening presence, with the smell of tobacco, gun oil, leather, and sweat, shouting orders in the harsh voices, slapping Manfred's face just for the fun of it, I forced myself not to cry, not to whimper in terror, but just to watch them as they made a list of what they were taking, with bureaucratic efficiency. The list wasn't to fool us into believing they might return the jewels, but to keep any of the soldiers from pocketing anything. "One pair of diamond earrings, one pearl necklace, one pair of silver cuff links, one gold watch and chain." Even my own few trinkets disappeared with that pile of jewels: a simple pin, a childish charm bracelet, a tiny gold ring.

In the ghetto, religious life fell apart. I hardly knew when it was the Sabbath. I can't remember any holidays. Yet Father prayed at home every morning. I do remember seeing him put on tefillin. The whole time he was in the ghetto he never rebelled against God, but I did. I looked for God, and I couldn't find Him. Where was justice in the world?

Somehow, without religious faith, we had to keep hoping. You never knew what the next day would bring. You expected the worst but hoped for a miracle. Liberation, barely imaginable, was too far off to count on, but somehow some of us managed to keep up some kind of hope, which gave us the courage to live.

Perhaps because I was a child, I don't remember hearing people talk about the war, at least not during the first two years in the ghetto. I do remember hearing about people who escaped from the ghetto, especially young men who tried to make their way to the partisans. But my family had no place to run. Manfred or I might have been able to escape individually, but we decided to stay together as a family. As far as I know, we weren't in contact with the underground. We just tried to get by.

The ghetto years were a time of great fear, constant fear. Every day people were killed. From time to time the Germans held *Aktionen* and assembled everyone in the ghetto. They announced on the loudspeaker that we were not to go out to work. Instead, everybody was to assemble in the great square on bare, trampled earth. We were lined up in long rows. The German soldiers strutted among us, making their switches whir as they cuffed people to make them stand straight, or for no reason at all. They went through the rows, separating people, sending Jews to the left or to the right.

They didn't announce that right was to work and left was to death. But we Jews knew. We stood in dread for long hours. The Nazis purposely split up families, to be cruel. Our family stood together. I forced myself to laugh and smile, to look as charming as I could, hoping my smiles would save us and keep us together. In fact, until the great Children's Action in 1944, we were fortunate. Except for Benno, we all stayed alive and together.

I swore an oath to myself in the ghetto, that I would do my best to encourage others and to live in hope. After the war, if I survived, I would help other people. I was full of ideas. People used to call me the girl wonder, *das Wunderkind.*

I kept myself going with dreams. I dreamt about the Land of Israel all the time. Even though I hadn't had a Zionist education, that was my dream. I visualized a family with children. I didn't have nightmares that I can remember. Every night I put myself to sleep with the dream that after the war we'd build a new house in the Land of Israel, and it would be full of children. I told my mother about my dreams. It was something to talk about. The dreams encouraged me. They gave me spiritual strength and the will to live. Without that, a person was liable to fall into a decline and die.

Children were especially vulnerable in the ghetto. Although I was small and might have passed for a younger child, I went out to work. I had to slave like an adult, because work was our only hope. We believed that the Nazis wouldn't kill productive workers, because they were fighting a war and needed our labor. Besides, if you didn't work, you didn't get a ration card, and without a ration card you couldn't get food—unless you stole it or bought it on the black market.

I was terrified the first morning I went to work. Fortunately, I was able to stay with my mother. I stood next to her among the rows of women at the gate, lined up by sixes. The guards searched us when we left, but not so carefully. The serious search came upon our return. They wanted to prevent us from smuggling anything into the ghetto. If they caught you with so much as a rotten potato, they'd kill you.

Nevertheless, whenever we left the ghetto on work details, we kept our eyes open for anything edible, a half-rotten turnip lying in a field, a crust of bread someone had thrown away—anything at all. We would snatch it up as swiftly as possible, without being seen by the guards. If we were too famished, we would devour the food on the spot, but we tried to control our own hunger and smuggle the food back into the ghetto for old and sick people, despite the danger which made us resourceful. We sewed secret pockets called *malines* in our clothes to conceal scraps of food, or anything else that might come in handy.

My grandparents were too old to work, and they depended on us. Although Jakob was a doctor, he did hard labor like anyone else.

We marched to work, a three-kilometer trek, summer and winter, and of course the Nazis didn't care whether we had decent clothes to protect us from the weather. We wore whatever was left over from the clothing we had brought to the ghetto with us.

We worked every day, except Sundays or when the Germans assembled us for an *Aktion*. The job I held the longest and remember best was at the German army hospital for wounded soldiers, the Kriegslazarett. The Kriegslazarett was in the countryside, beyond a village near Kovno where I had never been before. It was a stone building, three stories tall. I still have dreams about it sometimes.

The woman responsible for us was a German civilian, not a Kapo. About thirty Jewish women from the Kovno ghetto worked in that hospital, ten on each floor. There were a lot of advantages to working in the hospital. The work was indoors and the building was heated in winter, and on my floor the staff even gave the workers sandwiches. This was entirely exceptional. Two slices of fresh bread with a thin slice of greasy, third-rate sausage was an unheard of delicacy for us, the most tasty dish you could imagine. We were amazingly fortunate that the nurses in our department of the hospital had mercy on us. They could just as well have ignored our hunger or teased us with their food.

Our job in the hospital was to keep the bathrooms clean. We had to wipe up the most horrible filth: the spit, pus, and excrement of the patients. But at least we could wash ourselves at the end of the day. Sometimes, as I cleaned the toilets and urinals, I remembered my pampered childhood. I would look at my mother as she scrubbed the filthy porcelain. Once she had had maids to do the housework. What would they think if they knew that their former mistress was wiping toilet bowls for eight or nine hours daily?

I can't say exactly how long my mother and I worked in the hospital, only that it lasted many months. While we lived in the ghetto, stretches of time were not punctuated by special occasions and dates. Every day's fear and drudgery were like those of the day before, except when we learned of some new atrocity, when the Nazis selected yet another contingent of Jews for deportation and slaughter.

We had no contact with the patients, although occasionally a wounded soldier might wave to us or toss us a bit of food. I don't remember seeing an amputee or someone with his head bandaged and thinking, "Good for you! You got what you deserved! I wish the Russians had killed you!" But I prayed to the God in whom I no longer believed that the Germans would lose the war as quickly as possible.

The guards who marched us to work didn't stay with us all day long. They were regular troops, not like the SS who patrolled the ghetto and shot down Jews in cold blood. As much as I hated and feared the SS, I knew that not all the Germans were vicious criminals. But the soldiers who were not cruel were usually distant. A key to survival was picking out the ones who still had some remnant of a good heart, such as the nurses who gave us sandwiches at work. Sometimes I managed to catch a German soldier's eye. If I forced myself to smile sweetly, he might just throw me a crust of bread because I was cute. When that ploy worked,

I would snatch the bread from the ground, force myself to smile again, and thank him politely in my best German. But I always knew that the soldier who threw me bread could just as well have shot me if he had felt like it.

The soldiers often used to try to exploit the Jewish girls. They would pick someone out and walk to work next to her, unobtrusively making contact with her and offering to trade special favors for sex. My own upbringing had been strict, actually prudish. When I was a child I had never been told where babies came from, and I didn't dare ask. I knew that was something one simply didn't discuss. In Frankfurt, a certain Jewish woman had had an illegitimate child, and to this day I remember how everyone pointed their fingers at her in shame. When I heard that some girls in the ghetto were getting food for their families in return for sex, I wasn't at all tempted to try it, but the idea troubled me and I discussed it with Mother (not with Father, of course—he would sooner have died). To my astonishment, she didn't rule out the possibility entirely. If my life had truly depended upon it, I think she would have told me to go ahead. Luckily, it never came to that. I never suffered that particular degradation.

One young man did pay special attention to me, though. Every morning when I lined up to march to work, a certain soldier with a delicate, sensitive face always made sure to stand next to my line of six. He was a handsome young man in his mid-twenties, tall and thin, with light brown hair, blue eyes, and a long nose. He had a Jewish look underneath his German uniform.

I was diffident, but he soon made it clear that he had no sexual designs on me. He had just taken a liking to me, and he felt sorry for me. Very cautiously, so that no one would know or notice, he used to converse with me on the way to work. He said his name was Axel Benz and that his family had founded the Mercedes Benz company. He told me that one of his ancestors had been Jewish and that he felt sorry for the Jews. They were suffering unjustly, for they had done nothing wrong. He couldn't avoid joining the army, he explained, but he was a simple conscript, not an officer and not in the SS.

Axel Benz made my long, hard march to work more bearable. I came to look forward to his company. It was comforting to know that there was at least one kind Gentile in the world, even if he could do nothing to save us. He must have suffered terribly from loneliness among the coarse soldiers, afraid to tell anyone what was really on his mind.

Our friendship was of short duration. Axel Benz's unit was transferred to the eastern front. When he learned that he was leaving, Axel secretly gave me his gold watch, a very valuable one. He slipped it off his wrist when no one was looking, and I put it in a secret pocket inside my shirt.

"Perhaps you will be able to trade it for a lot of food," he said. "Maybe we'll see each other after the war."

At the ghetto gate, after he had escorted me to work for the last time, he gave me a look that said, "Just stay alive."

Amazingly enough, he did locate me after the war, and he actually offered to marry me! But we'll come to that.

I didn't have time to look carefully at Benz's watch. If anyone had seen him give it to me, that would have been the end of him, of me, and of the precious watch. I quickly hid it in my blouse. As I walked to work at the military hospital in the long column of ghetto women, I could feel the small, compact weight of the watch thumping against my chest.

The first chance I had, when my mother and I were alone cleaning the toilets, I took it out and showed it to her. Together we admired the astonishing present. It was so out of the ordinary that it was almost frightening, like a magic talisman.

We hadn't seen anything so fine since we had turned in all our jewelry. Benz's watch was very valuable. It would have been worth a fortune under any circumstances, but for Jews imprisoned in the ghetto, who owned almost nothing at all, it was undreamt-of wealth. The problem was that possession of jewelry was a capital offense. I had to keep it on my person, and if a guard caught me with it, I would be shot immediately, without question.

I couldn't take the risk of having it fall into anyone else's hands. Where could I hide it? The golden watch ticked so loudly that I half expected the sound to give me away. I had to get rid of the watch fast, though I so wished I could keep it. How long had it been since I had worn a pretty dress with a bracelet, a necklace, or a pin? I sneaked the watch past the guards on the way back into the ghetto, fearing that their probing hands would notice its hardness at my breast. When I got back home, I took it out and admired it.

I kept Benz's watch with me for a week, sleeping with it under my pillow of rags, wishing I could keep it forever. It meant so much to me because of what it was: it had been given to me by an enemy soldier, it was forbidden, and it was luxurious and came from another world, a world I had known before the war but one it was impossible to believe in from the perspective of the ghetto. I clung to Benz's watch as a sign of hope. Perhaps it meant I would live to see the end of the war. But it was dangerous to keep the watch, perhaps pointless.

Every day, on the way to work, we passed a small grocery store not far from the hospital. Not wanting to give up the watch, I decided, sadly and reluctantly, to bring it to that grocery shop and trade it for food. Obviously, we weren't allowed to ask our supervisors for permission to step out of the hospital for a few moments to go to the store. If I were caught sneaking out or sneaking in, at the very least I would be severely beaten. But the thought of the delicious food waiting for me in that store was overwhelming. I made a plan.

I usually wore a big, colored kerchief over my head. I could wrap it around my shoulders to hide the yellow stars on my chest and back, and then I could slip out of the hospital right under the guard's nose.

I didn't tell my mother exactly what I was planning. She knew, but I didn't ask for her permission. The watch was a God-sent opportunity and I couldn't waste it. I had to go, and she had to let me go. She would cover for me somehow if the supervisor happened to notice I was gone. I knew she would tremble with anxiety until I came back. I would be trembling too, but if that was the price, I was prepared to pay it and accept the risk.

Just getting out of the hospital took a bit of nerve. I slowly made my way down the stairway with a broom, sweeping the steps one by one, very thoroughly, at the same time keeping my eye out for Germans. The guard at the door was a sleepy, older man, and he paid no attention to the little Jewish cleaning girl with a scarf over her head. I kept sweeping the top steps, almost out of his sight, waiting until he was alone and looking the other way. Then I quickly hid the broom in a corner and pulled my mother's scarf down over my shoulders, hiding the Jewish stars on my clothes and letting my blond hair show. I simply walked by the guard, curtseying to him like a polite young Lithuanian farmgirl who had been visiting her soldier boyfriend in the hospital.

I stepped out onto the pavement, feeling like a free human being for the first time in a year or more, on my own outside the ghetto, not marked as a Jew. Of course, I was also terrified. My sense of freedom was entirely imaginary. I knew that. A sudden breeze might make my scarf flap and reveal the Jewish stars, and if I were caught, I would be beaten and then shot. They might also shoot my mother and all the other women on the hospital work detail. I tried not to think about those things.

I forced myself to walk slowly, as if I had all the time in the world, as if no one were looking over my shoulder, as if there were no danger all about me. I walked right past two soldiers. They called out to me in German, "Where're you going, sweetie?" I answered in Lithuanian, "To the store, sirs." They didn't bother me anymore.

Every day when we had marched by that store, my hungry stomach had regaled my imagination with images of what might be inside. I had dreamt of that store, of going in and pointing at everything that looked tasty and just gobbling it up: chocolates, cookies, cakes, rolls and butter. Now, at last, I would be going inside.

My hand shook as it pushed the door open. In my dreams the store had been endless, full of delicacies. In reality it was a simple grocery store. Even in peacetime it probably would not have had a particularly impressive selection of goods. Now, because of wartime shortages, its supply was especially meager. But for someone used to the ghetto, where a jar of jam was a treasure, that little grocery shop was like heaven. Just the smells were enough to make me giddy with pleasure, the fragrances of bread, oil, spices, vegetables, a couple of crude cheeses, and pickles floating in a barrel.

I fingered Benz's watch and looked over the goods. What was small enough and would keep well enough to hide, but was expensive enough to be worth trading the watch for? Until I walked into the store, I didn't know how hungry I was.

The storekeeper saw I was nervous, and he watched me with suspicion. I stood under his gaze, trying to look as calm as possible and rehearsing some sentences in Lithuanian: "I have no money, sir, but I want to trade something valuable for food."

"What do you have?"

"A gold watch."

"Let's see it."

Hesitantly, I took the watch out and showed it to the storekeeper. He grabbed it out of my hand.

"Where did you steal this?"

"I didn't steal it."

"How can I be sure? If the police catch me with stolen goods, I'll be in a lot of trouble."

It wasn't hard to see what was in the back of the

storekeeper's mind. He was a plump, bald man with a dirty white apron around his belly. His squinty eyes gave him away.

"Then give it back to me."

"Maybe I'll just keep it and turn it in to the police. There must be a handsome reward for a watch like this."

"My soldier friend gave it to me," I said. That part was true. The next part wasn't. "I'll tell him that you took it from me, and then you'll be sorry."

I made a couple of mistakes in Lithuanian as I spoke, but I had a German accent, and that must have made him a little unsure of himself. He mulled over my threat for a tense minute or two while I gazed at the food on his shelves and tried to ignore him. Finally, he said he'd give me some food for the watch.

I was ready to choose. I knew I would be cheated, no matter what. Benz's watch was probably worth more than everything in the store put together.

First I took three plump, white rolls and put them down on the counter. I picked out rice and sugar, honey, jam, and dried fruit—everything that looked relatively expensive, small, and sweet, until the storekeeper said, "That's enough, no more."

I bargained a little, forcing him to let me add some sweets. When I slipped as much of the food as I could into the secret pockets sewn into my clothes, the grocer must have guessed I was a Jew, but he didn't say anything. I tried not to think about the watch, the bright gold case, the delicate hands, the smooth ticking. It was degrading to have to trade such a gift just for food which would be eaten up in a day or two. A gift like that should have been saved forever. I left the shop, holding a few things in my hands.

Before I went back to the hospital, I crept around behind a building, where no one could see me. Petrified that I might be caught, the hunger was still too much for me. I took a small jar of honey and poured it out onto the roll. What a delicious moment! Despite my horrible fear, I ate as slowly as possible, to prolong that moment. My body was trying to grow, to fill out, to mature, and there was so little food to sustain it. I tried to feel the bread and honey as it reached every cell in my skinny little frame. "Run away," something in me said. "Don't go back to the hospital. Run away to the woods. Run away!" But how could I leave my mother in the hospital to face the fierce punishment my absence would bring?

My head was spinning with the joy of having a full stomach for once, and with the drunken feeling that freedom was possible. I didn't think I could stand straight if I got up. Gradually, I came to my senses again and cautiously headed back to the hospital.

The storekeeper did cheat me, because Benz's watch must have been worth twenty or thirty times the amount of food he gave me. Still, I had much more than I could eat by myself, and more than I could smuggle back into the ghetto in one trip.

I started thinking about where I'd hide the food in the hospital. I'd make a little storage place, and then every day I'd spirit some more back into the ghetto. But first of all, I'd fix a bread and honey sandwich for my mother. That morning I had borne the secret of the tiny, solid lump of Axel Benz's watch. Now I felt the hidden food rubbing against my body, and I imagined the pleasure it would bring my grandparents.

I drew near the hospital. It looked different now, larger and more threatening than it had looked in the morning when I had arrived with the crew of women workers. Then I had been anonymous, a little figure in a large group. Now I was the only one on the street, conspicuous.

From the outside I couldn't keep my eye on the lobby and choose the right moment to walk in. I walked past the hospital door once, trying to see in without being noticed. I continued on to the end of the block, then turned around and headed back. I decided to screw up my courage and walk right through the door, looking as breezy and self-confident as I could. I would curtsey to the guard, and if he asked me what I was doing there, I would answer in German. Perhaps I could make him think I was a Volksdeutsch girl. I imagined myself pushing open the door and smiling sweetly to the guard, and I made up a little speech to recite if he challenged me: "I want to visit my brave, wounded soldier friend." I even made up a name for myself, Kristina Schmidt.

I approached the hospital door again, and then I felt a heavy hand on my shoulder, fingers digging into the muscles till they hurt. I looked around in panic. Four soldiers had trapped me. "Where are you going, stinking Jew?" said the one who was gripping my shoulder.

Before I could recite my speech, saying, "I'm not a Jew. I'm Kristina Schmidt. I want to visit my brave, wounded soldier friend," my captor had lifted the scarf up, laying bare the yellow stars on my back and chest.

"Up to the hill with her," the leader said. Very roughly, without saying another word, they dragged me up a steep hill. When we reached the top, they threw me to the ground. A jar of jam rolled out of one of my secret pockets.

"You little sneak-thief," they shouted at me. They tore at my clothes and emptied my pockets. Standing over me and gloating, the German soldiers gobbled the precious food I had bought with Benz's watch, food I was planning to bring back for my grandparents in the ghetto. What they couldn't eat they poured out and scattered in the dirt.

"Stealing food, you filthy Jew-girl. We'll kill you for that," said the sergeant in charge. They plucked me off the ground and threw me against a wall. "You shoot her," the sergeant said to one of his men. The soldier stepped back and began to point his gun in my direction.

"Don't kill me!" I begged. "What did I do? I didn't steal that food."

"How did you get it then, you lying pig?"

I couldn't tell him the truth. If I told the story of Benz's watch, Benz would be killed, and so would I. German soldiers weren't allowed to talk to the Jews they were guarding, much less give them presents. If I said my father had kept a watch or some other valuable thing, that was forbidden, and my father could be killed for that along with me. Then I invented a story: "The storekeeper owed my father money from before the war."

"Blood sucking Jewish moneylenders, eh!"

I just hung my head and started reciting the Shema, the prayer a Jew is supposed to say with his dying breath. Then I started to cry. "Please let me go back to my mother," I begged them. "My mother and I work in the hospital. I just snuck out for ten minutes. I never did it before this. I swear I'll never do it again. Oh, please let me go!" I raised my eyes and looked at the soldiers, one by one, looking at their faces, especially the one who had been ordered to shoot me. "Have mercy on me," I begged, and I cried out to God, "Hear me, God!"

The one who had been appointed as executioner started raising his gun, but I could see he didn't want to shoot me. He looked toward his sergeant, and I looked at him too.

"We'll let you go, but just this once," the sergeant finally said. The soldiers dragged me back down the hill and up to the door of the hospital. The sergeant picked me up by the scruff of the neck and threw me in the door. I picked myself right up and raced upstairs to the floor where I was supposed to be working.

I wanted to cry. Nothing had gone right. I'd lost the watch and all the food, my clothes were torn, my body ached where the soldiers had gripped me and beaten me and thrown me down. I found Mother in one of the bathrooms on her knees, scrubbing the floor next to a urinal. I wanted to weep, but I had to kneel down next to my mother and wash the bathroom floor.

———

Some forced labor details in the ghetto were better than others. Our main criteria for judging forced labor were danger and the availability of food. At the military hospital we sometimes got extra food from the nurses, an amazing bonus. We were also sheltered, which was fine in the winter. But in the hot summer months the hospital was stuffy and oppressive. The smell of the festering wounds was unbearable. The filth in the bathrooms was twice as repulsive. The work was degrading and disgusting, and you constantly ran the risk of contracting an infection from contact with all the wounded soldiers' pus and excrement.

Sometimes, instead of sending us to work in the military hospital, they sent us out to work in the fields, and that too had both advantages and disadvantages. The work was much more tiring, and we were outdoors, at the mercy of the elements, but the supervision was more lax. We could talk, and we could filch potatoes or other food, if we were quick and resourceful. I became an expert on potatoes. I could tell when a bruised and rotten, filthy, abandoned scrap of root still had some nourishment in it. Today potatoes invariably remind me of the ghetto.

The fresh air roused my spirits, making me half forget my brush with death at the hands of roaming German soldiers. Sometimes we young people—we were really still children—could slip away from a work detail on a farm and steal fruit or food from other fields. The grown-ups were afraid to try it, but we weren't. From a distance we looked just like Lithuanian kids, and if we saw any soldiers we could just slip away. We went by ourselves or, at most, with one other kid. We were so hungry we would gobble up windfall apples, bruises and all. Kids are naturally daring. We developed a sixth sense to avoid patrols, to slip in and out of the groups of workers. It got to be a deadly kind of game. We had to keep an eye out for the guards, and the most frightening part, as always, was sneaking the stolen food back into the ghetto in our secret pockets.

The Nazis set up some small factories in the Kovno ghetto, and for a while I operated a machine that made silk stockings for women. It wasn't hard work, and I rather liked it. We didn't have to march long distances to work, it was indoors, we could sit, and we weren't under such strict guard. Those conditions made the work more dignified.

We always thought to ourselves: As long as we're useful to the Germans, they'll keep us alive. Food was scarce in the ghetto, but the workers were given soup and a piece of bread. We were slaves, but we clung to our dignity as long as we could. We knew that as long as they called us out in the morning and sent us off to work, there was hope that we would survive that day. That's how we lived, from day to day, hardly daring to hope for more than that we would live to the next day, that we wouldn't get sick, that the people we loved would be spared.

The fighting seemed far off. I didn't know much about what was going on. Occasionally, I would hear about a young man who ran away to the forests to try to join the partisans, but that was more a rumor than something real and present. The way I resisted was by clinging to life, and by dreaming of a rosy, romantic future: I would marry a rich man, and we would raise a huge family together in Palestine. We would eat rolls and butter and drink hot chocolate under a bright sun.

I tried to hold onto that bright sun in my imagination all the time. I saw how hard my parents were trying to keep their own spirits up, not to let themselves get discouraged, and I decided I would help them by being the "sun" of the family. I wouldn't make them sad by being sad myself.

In retrospect, I realize that only the absolute horror of the death camps made life in the ghetto seem close to some kind of normal state. I was young, and children are adaptable. But I was never reconciled to the way the Nazis forced us to live, densely crowded in a single room that was nothing like a home. Our poverty was unimaginable. We were reduced to a handful of patched and tattered garments, a few worn pieces of furniture and utensils, and hardly enough food to live on. I was hungry all the time, mad with hunger. It sometimes made me hallucinate.

The Nazis purposely designed our daily routine of hunger, dread, slave labor, and arbitrary killings in order to destroy our humanity, to reduce us to nothingness. In the world they made us live in, no action we took could give any meaning to our existence. Our work may have kept us alive, but it benefited the worst enemy the Jews have ever faced.

Danger never ceased lurking in the background, except when it leapt forward to occupy our entire existence. Disease was rampant in the ghetto. If you got sick, there were doctors but almost no medicine for treatment, and sick people didn't get food rations. Death became commonplace for me. A corpse was not a shocking sight anymore.

What weakened us the most, at least spiritually, was our complete isolation. The Nazis were committing crimes against us every minute of the day and night, unforgivable crimes, unprecedented crimes, and who was taking up our cause? There was no one to turn to for protection, no one to whom to protest about what was being done to us. The Allies may have been fighting Hitler, but they weren't making any effort to save us. We had been forgotten.

Of all of us, my father knew the most about what was

going on. He worked as a clerk at the Judenrat, and he knew about the horrible decisions that the Jewish leadership had to make. Perhaps he discussed these things with my mother, but I never got wind of them. Father continued working with quiet courage, keeping up his daily routine of prayer and observance as much as he could, and giving us strength. He drew faith from his prayers. It was a deep, personal faith now, nothing I could ask him about.

In the past, Father had always been resourceful, constantly seeking escape routes for us. He had gotten us out of Nazi Germany and Nazi-occupied Memel, and he had saved us from being sent to Siberia by the Russians. But there was nothing he could do to get us out of the ghetto. He had always been master of his own destiny; now he was reduced to helpless, passive subordination. Yet he never betrayed his frustration to me. To me, he remained himself, a strong, loving father, until the very last.

The ghetto progressively emptied. The Nazis killed us one by one and in masses. The largest and most vicious mass killing, an *Aktion*, took place quite early, on October 28, 1941.

Obviously, the Nazis didn't announce that they were going to kill ten thousand of us. They said they were going to separate the working people from those unfit to work, and the latter would be sent to a special facility so that food rations could be distributed more equitably.

We were not sent out to work on the day of the *Aktion*. Instead, everyone in the ghetto, without exception, had to assemble in a large, open square, the Democratu Plaza. About twenty-eight thousand people began crowding into the plaza at five in the morning, when it was still very chilly and dark. No one took the chance of hiding inside. We had been warned that the Nazis would make a house-to-house search, and anyone found at home would be shot. The plaza was surrounded by German troops and Lithuanian partisans.

By late October in Lithuania, the weather is already very cold and wintry. The days are short, and they can be damp and nasty. October 28 was bitter cold. We lined up in columns, and the Nazis began marching us past a single German officer, one man who decided the fates of nearly thirty thousand human beings. With small motions of his hands he sent us either to the right or the left. Right meant life; left, we knew, meant death. Right was supposed to mean work, food rations, and a form of security, but, in fact, being fit for work had very little to do with the direction we were sent. There were too many of us for a careful selection. The officer just sent people whichever way he wished, and we could see he was purposely breaking up families. He obviously enjoyed hearing screams of anguish as parents were wrenched away from their children and wives from their husbands.

The day dragged on, and columns slowly advanced past the officer. Sick and old people collapsed in the plaza, and no one was allowed to help them. Babies and young children wept as they became so cold and hungry that they couldn't bear it any longer. I watched, and my heart ached, but we were helpless, unable to do anything for the others, and full of dread about our own fate. As we moved forward toward the selection point my fear grew more and more intense. I could barely feel the cold any longer. I wasn't hungry. I concentrated on the approaching moment, when my fate would be decided by a German officer's hand motions: right or left, life or death, hope or despair.

Our family drew closer, Father, Mother, Manfred, and I, my mother's parents and her brother Jakob—Benno had already been murdered. If the selection had been systematic my grandparents would have had no hope of surviving it, since they were really too old to work. But because it was arbitrary, I prayed silently that somehow the officer might have mercy on them.

Mercy was hardly a concept with which the Nazis were familiar. But I said to myself, if we smiled confidently and walked erect, perhaps we would pass. So I forced myself to smile, and I called softly to my grandparents, "Stand up straight and walk with pride, and they won't send you to the left."

Did it work? Is that why they passed through? Is that why our family remained together? I want to believe it. I have always tried to control my destiny and force things to come out the way I want them to, even when facing the Nazis. They might have had physical power over us, but I resolved to do whatever I could. If something so small as a smile and a sparkle in my eye could save my life and help pull my family through, I was going to find the courage and spirit to force myself to smile, to will myself through the selection. It wasn't so much that I was frightened of where I might be sent as that I couldn't bear the idea of being separated from my family.

That afternoon my family left the plaza alive and still united, but ten thousand people were sent to the left. They were all shot, out of town at the Ninth Fort. Ten thousand people were snatched away from the ghetto. And that was only the beginning of the slaughter.

Because of the dreadful conditions in the ghetto—hunger, cold, overwork, disease, and hopelessness—many of the Jews who hadn't been rounded up and shot in the huge *Aktion* of October 28 gradually died of hunger and various illnesses. A few younger Jews ran away to join the partisans, and the Nazis sent others off in trains, in trucks, and by foot. We never heard from them again.

For those of us who remained after the selections and actions and transports, even though the Nazis kept making the area of the ghetto smaller, the ghetto was less oppressively crowded with living souls. Now the streets teemed with the memory of people who were no longer there.

After some time we moved out of the room in the tenement block where we first settled and into a kind of detached house with my grandmother and grandfather. The house wasn't big, but it had a small yard. Even though Grandmother and Grandfather didn't go out to work, we managed to keep them alive. Somehow they managed to pass through all the selections. My uncle Jakob was working, and he brought them food. So did the rest of us.

My brother, Manfred, got married in the ghetto. There may have been a very modest, minimal religious ceremony, but there was certainly no celebration, not like my aunt Tita's wedding back in Memel. It was safer for people to live as couples. They had more strength together. It also helped with the Germans. To some extent, they spared married people.

Even I had a touch of romance in my life. A redheaded boy I knew used to stand under my window and sing me serenades. He said he'd marry me after the war, but I told him I could never marry him because his hair was too red. That young man did survive the war, and now he lives in America. I'm still grateful to him for his songs. They gave me just a bit more courage and strength to keep a grip on life. It helped to know that someone cared for me. Somehow young people remembered to act young. Even in the dismal horror of the ghetto, we didn't give up hope entirely.

On March 27, 1944, the day before my father's birthday, we went to work as usual. Mother and I trudged out to the army hospital and spent all day cleaning the bathrooms. For us it was an uneventful day. But back in the ghetto, as we learned when we returned from work, it had been far from uneventful. The Nazis had begun rounding up all the remaining children.

After everybody who was fit for work had left, German soldiers went from house to house and announced that all the children had to gather in the square, with the mothers who had stayed behind to mind them. No one doubted for a moment that this was a death sentence. Not everybody went out to the square. Some mothers had planned in advance for a moment like this, and they desperately tried to hide their children. They had built hiding places in the walls or false bottoms in cupboards. But the Nazis ransacked the apartments, and there wasn't one single child whom they didn't find. When we returned from work, we could feel the grief clinging to the doors and windows. The air of the ghetto was stained with bitter anguish.

What could the mothers do? They wanted to go with their children and try to save them, and they also wanted to stay alive themselves. They had other loved ones to protect, other children, husbands, and parents. They had to watch as their young children were torn from them. Thinking they had a choice, they tried to make up their minds right there, on the spot, with no chance to ask anyone or leave a message for anyone. What was the "right" decision? Should they go with their young children or remain behind with the rest of their families?

In fact, their bitter choice didn't matter, because, with special cruelty, the Germans made a point of doing exactly the opposite of what the women wanted. If a mother wanted to go wherever her children were sent, she was beaten and pushed away, and the ones who didn't want to go with their children were seized and dragged away with them.

The next day, my father's birthday, March 28, 1944, we had to go to work again. What a fearfully hollow feeling we had as we left the ghetto that morning! We all knew some of the children who had been taken away and killed. They were our brothers, our cousins, or our nieces and nephews. Even if they were just children we had seen playing in a yard, their blood was ours. We looked down at the ground as we trudged along, afraid to glance at a window and catch a bereaved mother's eye. Every house where there had been children the day before was now flooded with grief. Those with children still inside trembled with horrible dread. The Nazis hadn't been able to round up all the children the day before, and no one doubted that the soldiers would go on with their vicious work.

I was just over the borderline separating children from those old enough to work, so my life would be spared.

This selection would pass me by. Overcome by grief for others, one clung most tightly to one's own family. Father embraced me with extra warmth that morning as he saw me leave the house. We congratulated him on his birthday, praying that we would all be liberated before his next one.

All day long, as I worked in the hospital, I thought about what had happened the day before, the dreadful scenes that had been described to me, mothers weeping to the soldiers, shouting, "Don't take my child from me!" I imagined the violence of soldiers smashing down doors, slapping down mothers who tried to protect their children, brutally beating and shoving the children. I knew it was happening while we worked in the hospital. How angry I felt, how helpless, how vulnerable!

On the way home that day we walked listlessly. We didn't want to get back to the ghetto and find out what had happened, to hear about more mothers and children who had been dragged away to death.

When we reached home, Father wasn't there. Mother rushed out to the Judenrat office and found a Jewish policeman. She begged him to tell us what had happened to Father, and this is what she learned.

Father had devised a secret plan. In a storage attic under the roof of the Judenrat offices, he had gathered a large number of older children, perhaps as many as a hundred. He must have thought the Nazis wouldn't search that building, or that the members of the Judenrat would be able to intervene with the authorities and save the children if they were found. He obviously hoped that once the *Kinderaktion*, the Children's Action, was over, any child still remaining in the ghetto could join us at work.

This was not an impulsive, improvised act, but a carefully planned operation. It had to be, in order to gather the children secretly and get them to the building in the middle of the night. Of course, Father hadn't told us of his plan. Mother could never have borne the tension, knowing that her husband was risking his life. Quietly, calmly, he had done what he thought was right, but he and the children had been discovered.

The Nazis took all of them, the children and my father, to the Ninth Fort on a tall hill outside of the ghetto. Mother begged the Jewish policeman to go there and try to save Father. He rushed off, but before he could get there, the Nazis had killed everyone with machine guns. That's what he told us when he came back.

Two thousand children were murdered during the *Kinderaktion*. Those children were our hope for the future, the ones who had remained alive for almost three years, despite everything, and now they were all dead. While the children had been alive we could pray and hope that we might survive and rebuild our lives. After the children were murdered, what hope was there for the adults? Their deaths made me feel a hundred years old. I no longer belonged to the generation of children. I was an adult.

Father didn't have to try to save the children. He should have known it was hopeless. But that was like him, always doing more for other people than for his own family. Now we needed him desperately.

Until Father was killed, Mother acted like a heroine. She never let me feel how much she was suffering. There had been days when I wanted to quit everything. On our way to work, as I walked along next to her, we would speak softly, so the guards couldn't overhear us. Conversation was forbidden. You could be killed for talking.

Still I would whisper, "I'm going to break out of line and run into the woods. I don't care if they shoot me. I can't work like this for the rest of my life."

She would grab my hand, afraid I would carry out my threat. "Don't let yourself be shot dead for nothing."

"I don't care!" I would tell her. I was in my early teens, supposed to be growing up into womanhood, and what future did I have? But Mother encouraged me. She reassured me. I wouldn't have to do disgusting work in an army hospital all my life. The war would end. The Nazis would lose. We would be freed together if we stayed together. In the hospital she managed to keep going. She doggedly cleaned up the wounded Nazi soldiers' disgusting phlegm and pus, and she didn't show that she felt humiliated.

But after my father was killed, Mother was half herself. Everything suddenly changed. Mother didn't want to live any longer. She aged forty years after he was murdered. I saw I had to take charge. But where would I get the energy, the will, and the courage? Strangely enough, it came, the moment I needed it.

We had to keep on working. The Nazis gave their victims no time off for grief, no consideration for bereavement. My mother's beloved husband of more than twenty years was shot one day, and the next day she had to march out to the Kriegslazarett to clean up the wounded soldiers' filth. Suddenly I had lost my father, a man I admired absolutely, whose presence gave me guidance in life—and now I had to find the strength that my mother couldn't find at first, the power to go on.

Father had been the dominant figure in our family, and Mother and I had naturally deferred to him, counted on him, needed him. Now that he was gone, we both had to learn to live on our own.

My mother and I were like two exhausted swimmers caught in a flood. Whenever one of us went under, the other had to find the strength to pull her head above water. At the start I came to the surface and caught my breath first. It was slightly easier for me, because I was younger and more resilient.

I saw immediately that I was the only thing that kept Mother alive, and I knew that without her I couldn't live. Mother and I had only each other, and right after Father was killed, I was the one who had to become more responsible, more active.

Neither my mother nor I could find that strength in religion any more. All his life Father had been a truly religious man, not just an observant one. He had maintained himself with his faith during the most trying circumstances, under impossible conditions. He had lost everything he had worked for and built up all his life, but he had always faced adversity with courage and had never given up his belief.

I cannot forget how he looked every morning, in our dreadful, crowded little room, praying devoutly in his white prayer shawl and tefillin. Faith in God had sustained my father while he lived in the ghetto, but I could no longer believe in Him after He let my father be killed.

Before Father was killed, when we were at work, my mother had spared me the hardest, filthiest jobs. But in the days immediately afterward, she was too stunned to manage, and I did the work for both of us. Later Mother recovered somewhat, and we became equal partners in the project of survival.

We sacrificed ourselves for each other. A lot of people might talk about self-sacrifice, but we really did it. She realized that because of her I had someone to live for. And I knew that because of me, she had someone to live for.

There was no school for me in the ghetto, but I got a kind of education, an education in strength and self-reliance. Before the ghetto, I had always been well dressed and had never known hunger. I had never had to work except at my lessons in school. Perhaps the only thing that prepared me for life in the ghetto was my sense of determination. Whatever the situation, I had always set about overcoming any obstacles. Nothing was going to get the worst of me. I had always been strong-willed, and my parents had valued that in me.

My childhood stopped abruptly in 1941. When I emerged from Jonas's meat freezer with my family, I had stopped being a child, but I certainly wasn't ready to be a grown-up. After that time, when I visualize myself, I don't think of myself getting older—not in the normal sense of adding one year to another. The ghetto deformed my development. I no longer celebrated birthdays or moved up from grade to grade, marking orderly progress toward becoming an adult.

Three years passed in the ghetto. Physically, I remained small and undeveloped. My body never had enough food to grow properly. And every day during those three years my mind had to struggle with absurd cruelty, and my heart had to live with monstrous fear and grief. Three years passed in the ghetto, but inside myself I fought to stay the same, to remain the little girl I had been in 1941. I laughed at myself for being attached to a doll, but I clung to Leslie, the doll I had brought all the way from Frankfurt. I tried to cling to memories of my childhood: my mother's piano, the appliqué dresses she always wore, my father's pipe, his black satin yarmulke, the red Jewish star on Candy's cap. Perhaps that was the only way I had of preventing my soul from being damaged beyond all repair.

The war felt utterly endless. We didn't know whether Jews would ever be able to live as free, normal people again. Three years went by, but it could have been forever. I aged by half a century.

The last few months of the ghetto were the worst. We were all stricken by grief. Conditions deteriorated. Food became even scarcer. The Germans worked us harder. But we knew they were losing the war. The summer of 1944 came. The Allies landed in Normandy. There were encouraging rumors. We overheard conversations among the Germans. The Red Army was approaching, and we had something to hope for.

If we could just survive from day to day, we might live to be liberated by the advancing Russian troops. We knew that the Germans would try to liquidate the ghetto before they left it behind. Our problem would be to avoid being killed or deported until the Russians arrived. Jakob began preparing for the end. He constructed a bunker in the basement of our house where we could hide.

The army hospital where we were working kept receiving new batches of wounded soldiers. That was encouraging for us on two counts. It was good to see that the enemy was taking a beating, and we expected that as long as we were needed to maintain the hospital, the Germans would keep us alive.

Then on July 8, 1944, they began rounding up all the remaining Jews in the ghetto and shipping us out on trains. This time there was no selection. Everybody went.

The end of the ghetto came all at once. Without warning, the Germans attacked the ghetto. They summoned us all out of our houses and announced that everyone who stayed behind would be rounded up and killed. Meanwhile, we could hear the Russian shelling in the distance, an encouraging sound but a terrifying one.

We had only two agonizing choices: to report to the plaza voluntarily and be marched to the trains, or to try to hide. We didn't know where they would send us, but we did know that if they caught us hiding, they might shoot us on the spot. My mother's brother Jakob and her parents decided to take their chances in the bunker he had made.

"We're too old," my grandfather said, and I knew he was right. Wherever the Germans sent us, there would be selection after selection, and the old people would be the first to be killed. But I was young, and Mother wasn't that old. We could pass through the selections and keep working. We could live. If Jakob came with us, he could live too. But Jakob decided to stay with his parents and hope they could evade the German searches.

They announced on loudspeakers that the Jews had to report to the plaza. Mother and I said a last farewell to

Jakob and my grandparents and left them behind in the house. Perhaps they would survive. We could always hope. We had to.

We were not allowed to bring anything with us when we left the ghetto. I left Leslie, that last fragment of my childhood, under my bed. Perhaps after the war I would come back and find her.

We assembled at the plaza, and the Germans marched us down to the railroad depot. I don't remember that I was exactly frightened. Part of me, perhaps, was glad to be leaving the ghetto, feeling, mistakenly, that nothing could be worse than that confinement. Mostly, I guess, I was numb from so much loss: no father, no grandparents, no uncle, no house, no belongings. I clung to my mother. Manfred and his wife marched along in the crowd, too.

At the train platform there were a lot of soldiers. They screamed and hit us, shouting orders, intimidating us. There was confusion and panic, but everything moved very fast. They separated the men and the women and loaded us onto the trains within a few hours. Manfred was swept off with the other men before my mother and I could say goodbye to him. Dita, his wife, was heartbroken, but we parted from her too. We didn't understand why they separated the men and the women: just another instance of gratuitous cruelty, we supposed, if we had the mental energy to suppose anything.

The Germans counted us off and crammed us into cattle cars, filthy and unventilated. It was a hot July day. We had no water to drink. Just waiting in the stationary cars under the blazing sun was torture. Finally, at night, they attached a locomotive to the cattle cars, and it pulled us away from

Kovno. Through slats in the side of the car I could see parts of the ghetto burning. There were no fires in the area where my grandparents' house stood. Perhaps they would survive.

From the Labor Camp to the Crematorium

CHAPTER FOUR

From the flaming Kovno ghetto the train brought us to the Stutthof concentration camp, where I was separated from my mother during the selection. It was during that first stopover at Stutthof that I crossed over to the side of those condemned to the gas chambers, changed clothes with my mother, and brought her back with me to join those who were healthy enough to be worked to death rather than gassed and burned. After the selection, the Nazi guards lined us up in columns at the gate of the concentration camp and prepared to send us to labor camps in the Polish countryside. There, within the next few months, most of us would die of exposure, exhaustion, hunger, or disease. I couldn't know it at the time, but my mother and I were going to be sent back to Stutthof, and no trick that I might devise could save our lives.

Now, at the gate of the concentration camp, after I had slipped through the cracks in the Nazis' vicious order and managed to keep my mother with me, we stood silently side by side in the column of women. I didn't recognize anyone around me. Nobody talked. We stood and waited. Behind us the selection went on. We could hear the women's scuffling footsteps, their sobs as they were separated from their loved ones, the guards' angry shouts as they shoved the women to their fate. Gates clanged shut. Occasionally, a dog snarled.

Silently, I took inventory of what was left to me: a pair of wooden clogs, somebody else's clothes, and my mother. Both of us were extremely weak. We were exhausted from the ordeal we had just gone through, and we hadn't many reserves of strength to draw upon. We had hardly eaten anything at all since being driven out of the Kovno ghetto. Of course, we hadn't been able to sleep comfortably in the crowded cattle car that had taken us from there. The floor of the train had been covered with excrement. Women had collapsed and lain on it, dying of exhaustion and suffocation. We had arrived at Stutthof in a state of mental, physical, spiritual, and moral exhaustion, which had left us virtually no energy to withstand the violence done to us during the preparations for the selection and the selection itself. Now we were being worn down further.

Hopeless and despairing, we waited in the sun. It took them a long time to gather enough of us for their purposes. Heavily armed guards stood on both sides of our columns, as if we exhausted women had the power to stage a rebellion against the German army. Just standing in line was enough to wear some of the women out.

The guards watched us indifferently, but I knew they might suddenly erupt into violence. I was afraid my mother might collapse and fall down in a faint. If she did, the Kapos would rush over and beat her to death where she lay. Earlier that morning I had seen a Kapo trample a woman to death for the fun of it.

The incident had taken place in the huge hangar where they had issued clothing to us. The Kapos, German women in uniform, circulated among us to make sure we went about our business as quickly as possible and to keep us from removing anything we might have hidden in the lining of our old clothes and transferring it to a new hiding place. One of the prisoners, a woman of about thirty, had asked the Kapo a question. I didn't hear what she said. It probably wasn't anything sarcastic or impertinent— though I hope it was, considering what happened to her. Without warning the Kapo swung her arm around, putting the whole force of her stocky body into the blow. She struck the prisoner cruelly on the neck, knocking her to the ground. Then while the prisoner squirmed and groaned, trying feebly to protect herself with her arms, the Kapo jumped up and down on her body. At first the prisoner screamed and howled in agony, but soon she was silent and unconscious. After the prisoner was dead, the Kapo pushed the body with her foot, turning it over. She looked about her with a satisfied smile and carefully dusted off her boots, wiping them on the dead woman's clothing.

Then she summoned two other prisoners. Terrified, they approached her. "Take away this filth," she ordered them. They didn't dare ask her where to take the body. They just picked it up by the feet and shoulders and carried it out somewhere. In a moment the bloody spot on the earth where the prisoner had been murdered was trampled over by hundreds of pairs of feet, and there was no longer any sign of the crime, except the awful fear in the hearts of those of us who had seen it.

"Mother," I whispered. "We have to be strong now. We have to hold onto life." She looked at me wanly. "Mother," I spoke again. "The two of us. We're going to live."

Finally, after who knows how much time, they marched us forward, out of the camp gates to the railroad siding, and forced us into cattle cars again, shoving us into the same filthy cars that had brought Jews to Stutthof. No one cleaned them out except to remove the corpses.

After they closed and locked the doors, some of the prisoners speculated about where the Germans might be taking us. Once the train began to move they tried to figure out which direction we were going, as if knowledge could give us some kind of control over our situation, as if knowledge were a key to survival. We didn't know whether we would be traveling for a day or a week or only a couple of hours. The horror of uncertainty was almost more frightening than the specter of certain death, which we had just faced in the concentration camp.

That evening, after riding south for a few hours, they took us out of the train near the Polish city of Torun, also known as Thorn. They divided up the women on the train and sent them to a number of smaller labor camps. The camps had no facilities. We slept outdoors on the ground in all weather, two together under a single, thin blanket. We had to wash in buckets and barrels and relieve ourselves in ditches. We wore the same clothes day after day until they were caked with sweat and dirt, which held together better than the thin threads they were woven of. The only food we got was filthy potato-peel soup. I still feel grit on my teeth when I think about that soup.

My mother and I were sent to make tank emplacements for the defense of the city against the advancing Russian army. This was harder work than we had ever done. Still, as in the ghetto, I tried to march to work with a smile on my face. Despite the dreadful suffering, I did my best to find some way of enjoying life: a bit of warmth from the sun, a stem of grass to suck on, a dream. We had no hope, but I forced myself to hope, and I encouraged the other prisoners to look cheerful, too.

The Germans made the work as difficult and strenuous as they could. Using picks and shovels, we had to dig deep pits in the earth and smooth them around the edges. My mother didn't have the strength for digging, but I was a good worker. The tank emplacements were three or four meters deep. To spare my mother, I took the hardest work. I had to stand at the bottom of the pits and throw shovelfuls of dirt far up over my head. Just a small girl, I worked in the shadow of those high walls, with the guard, armed with his machine gun, standing on the top and grinning to see what a strain it was. The Kapo enjoyed seeing me suffer. He seemed to be standing on top of a mountain, looking down at me as I threw shovelful after shovelful of earth up over the rim. I barely had the strength to lift my arms, let alone the shovel, heavy with soil. But because I was such a good worker, the guards gave my mother a much easier job: smoothing and packing the earth on top of the pits. By working well I also earned an extra bowl of soup every day, which I shared with my mother. I wasn't working for the Germans, I was working for her.

Days had not been so long since we were in Jonas's meat freezer. They woke us up at dawn with shouts and blows, and then we had to line up and be counted. There weren't many of us, about a hundred, but the morning count could still take a long time if the guards felt like toying with us. Then they marched us out to the fields where we were digging the tank emplacements. We had to walk several kilometers each way. Here no one talked to me kindly the way Benz had on the marches to work from the ghetto. Every day was like the one before. The deeper we dug, the farther we had to fling the dirt. My arms and back ached from morning till night, and all night long as well. With empty bellies we went to sleep on dry weeds piled up to cushion the bare ground, sleep that couldn't possibly restore our strength.

We marked the passing hours with strokes of our picks, swinging shovels, dirt moved from place to place. The Nazis made us work fast—otherwise we would be beaten—and we had to learn tricks to save energy. We had to learn to rest between strokes without looking as though we were resting. As we dug, we prayed that those defenses wouldn't work against the Red Army when it came to liberate Torun. We prayed. Let the Red Army come like a raging fire and destroy every German tank in its path.

The days passed slowly with our exhausting drudgery. There was never enough food, so we grew thinner and weaker, and the work got harder for us. Each day was endless, and yet the days went by too fast because the cold autumn was approaching, and then the ferocious Polish winter.

Friendships among the prisoners didn't develop very much. There were few outward signs of solidarity. No one had the strength for that. We were like weary animals, thinking only about how to get a little more food, a little more rest, how to avoid being beaten. We slept outside on the ground, making crude cushions out of dry weeds, with one rough blanket for two people. The camp was on a hill, without a fence, but there was nowhere to escape. We were in the midst of hostile territory. The Kapos had a tent, and every night they sat around a big bonfire. They wanted us to see and smell how well they were eating while we went hungry.

The Kapos were chosen because of their cruelty. That seemed to be their main qualification. The one who supervised the guards was a real murderer. You learned very quickly to stay out of his way. All the Kapos enjoyed seeing us suffer. They wore us down and tortured us until we collapsed and died.

I was hungry all the time. Every night I used to dream about eating a roll and butter and drinking a hot cup of cocoa—such vivid dreams! I had as much food as I wanted in my dreams, cup after cup of thick, hot cocoa, and crisp rolls with lots of butter. Those dreams could not have contrasted more strongly with the tiny amounts of terrible food we were given. The main staple was the watery soup made of filthy potato peels, so dirty that I could feel the grit between my teeth as I drank it. They cooked the soup in the camp and brought it to us.

Luckily, I was still a cute young girl. Occasionally, by smiling sweetly, I could get a soldier to take pity on me and throw me a crust of bread. Half a sandwich was a vast treasure there. I used to share those lucky bonuses with my mother. Just as in the ghetto, some of the women slept with the Kapos to get extra food and favors. Although my mother obviously didn't approve of that, she let me know that I could do it too if it would save my life, but the idea sounded awful to me. I resolved that I wouldn't do it unless I had absolutely no other hope at all.

Despite the savage cruelty of our life in the labor camp, the fear and degradation, the physical suffering and hunger, I absolutely wanted to keep on living. I had endurance, and I helped myself to bear the suffering with dreams and prayers. I struggled to keep my mother's spirits up, and I never let hope die within me.

Sometimes news filtered in that the Russians were advancing. But why so slowly? We hoped that rescue would come. It was a blessing to be able to maintain hope. Hope could keep you alive. Anger also gave us strength. We were angry at the world. Where was everybody? How long was it going to take before the Allies defeated the Nazis? We knew the Nazis were going to lose the war one day, and we clung to our lives in order to see that future day.

The months went by and the weather grew colder. We saw no signs of the Russians drawing nearer. The winter was approaching. Even in early autumn the cold, damp wind penetrated our thin clothing. We might as well have been naked. There was no shelter but an improvised shed, nowhere to wash. The merciless wind made our skin red and chapped. The skin cracked and dirt sank into the cracks. It was painful to bend our fingers.

We prisoners had almost nothing to talk about with each other. If it hadn't been for my mother, I would have been all alone. The loneliness would have weakened me as much as the work and the starvation. Having someone to care for me and someone for me to care for gave both of us strength to go on.

We were nowhere, abandoned, digging huge holes in an enormous plain in complete isolation from the rest of the world. We were emaciated. We staggered rather than walked. I remember looking at the other slave laborers and wondering how they managed to stand up and when they were going to die. I must have looked the same, but I didn't have a mirror in which to see myself. Mostly, I was concerned about my mother, praying that she would stay healthy and strong. I had to keep her spirits up by talking about the future, how we would live happily after the war was over. I was sturdier than she was, and I tried to spare her as much hardship as I could.

The Nazis didn't give us a quarter of the food we needed to sustain life, but they demanded a full quota of hard work from us. We got weaker and weaker. When a woman got too weak or fell ill with no chance of recovery, they sent her back to Stutthof by train to be gassed and cremated. Deaths were a daily occurrence.

Everything became much harder to do in the cold. The handles of the tools were freezing and rough. The tools felt heavier every day. We no longer had the strength to grasp and swing them properly. The only good thing about work was that when you were down inside a tank emplacement, you were sheltered from the wind.

When it rained the earth turned to thick mud, so heavy you could barely lift it up to remove it from the deep pits. All day long we worked under the cold rain, wearing nothing but our thin prison clothes, standing in mud up to our ankles or calves. The mud clung to our clogs and kept pulling them off. When the rain stopped, we would be grateful for a little warmth from the sun, if the wind wasn't too fierce, but when the earth dried it turned cold and hard, like concrete, making it doubly hard to dig.

One sunny day I swung my pick down with all my might to break the crusted earth, but fatigue put me off my stroke, and the pick hit my leg and dug into it. The pain knocked me down. My mother saw what had happened to me and turned to rush down into the pit to help me.

"Where are you going, pig!" shouted the Kapo, pointing his gun at my mother.

"My daughter, my daughter is hurt," she answered. She didn't stop running toward me, down the side of the pit.

She only had time to look briefly at my leg. The Kapo screamed at her: "Get back up and work, you filth." Then he pointed at me. "You," he said, "back on your feet! No idleness!"

My mother helped me to my feet, but I could hardly stand. It didn't feel as if a bone were broken, but my leg was bleeding. It started swelling almost immediately. My mother slowly went back to her place. Her face looked sadder than I'd ever seen it.

"You, start working," the Kapo shouted at me.

"Please, sir, just let me rest a minute. My leg is badly hurt," I begged him. If I hadn't been known as a hard worker, the Kapo would have shot me then and there. As it was, he hardly gave me any time to rest. I couldn't clean or bandage the wound. They forced me to keep working all that day.

That night I could barely sleep because of the pain. But

the fear was much worse than the pain. Serious injury was a death sentence. I couldn't let this happen to me.

When we woke up, my mother asked me anxiously, "How is it?" We examined my leg. It looked horrible. I could hardly bear to look at it. My calf was swollen. The skin was discolored. It hurt me dreadfully, but of course I forced myself to get up.

I limped to the morning roll call and then, after they had counted and insulted us as usual, I limped over to eat what passed for breakfast: one cup of lukewarm, watery stuff, which they claimed was imitation coffee, and a small slice of hard, dry, badly baked bread. Then we lined up to march to work. I realized I could not possibly walk three or four kilometers across rutted, muddy fields. I sank to the ground and wept. This was the end for me.

They let me rest that day, but, naturally, they cut my rations back to one bowl of soup now that I wasn't productive anymore. One day of rest wasn't enough, of course. When my mother came home from work that evening, she didn't have to ask me how I felt. I was moaning with the pain.

Time dragged by. Was it a day or two or a week? I don't know. I was too sick to keep track of time. It's astonishing that they didn't do away with me then and there. Maybe it was because I had been such a hard worker before. Maybe it was because I was still just a girl and always tried to be cheerful, even forcing myself to smile at the vicious monsters who were guarding us. I don't know why, but they let me lie in the shed and try to get better. Once or twice a guard who was less evil than the others even gave me an extra piece of bread with a scrap of cheese or sausage. No treasure in the world could possibly have approached the value of a half-eaten sandwich at that time.

The other prisoners were concerned about me. Everybody had some suggestion, but nothing worked. The cut was infected, and my calf filled with pus, growing enormous and turning red, black, and blue. The swelling was grotesque. My leg, like my whole body, had been reduced to skin and bones, so I looked like a skeleton with a heavy bag full of water tied behind its knee. I was running a high fever, and I was too delirious and incoherent to be frightened anymore. My mother left for work every morning full of dread. She didn't know whether she would find me there when she came home. She lay at my side and cried bitterly, and I had to calm her down.

One day a Nazi doctor showed up in our shed and examined my leg. The Kapos certainly didn't bring him specially to treat me. He must have been on some kind of inspection tour or else maybe treating one of the Kapos, so they took him over to see what he could do for me.

The doctor resembled any other Nazi officer, clean, stiff, proud, and nasty. With an abrupt motion he pushed the filthy blanket aside, using his swagger stick so he wouldn't have to touch it with his own hands. He examined my leg from a distance, without touching it. The dreadful stench of the pus made him twist his lip in disgust, but otherwise his face was expressionless. Then, with no warning, he slipped a pocketknife out of his pocket, opened it, and lanced the sore. He cut right into my living flesh. The pain filled my entire body and blinded me for a moment. Pus and blood poured out of the wound onto the straw beneath me. The doctor had to step back and turn his head away because I stank so much.

The pain took a long while to die down, but I didn't dare scream out loud. If I screamed, the Nazi doctor might get annoyed at me, pull out his pistol, and shoot me in the head. That's something I'd seen happen often enough, even in the ghetto. Without a word, the Nazi meticulously wiped the blood and pus off the blade of his pocketknife, folded it, and put it back in his pocket. "I must remember to disinfect this," he mumbled to himself. Then he turned on his heels and left me on my filthy platform in the shed, still shaking with fever. My leg was throbbing, exploding, radiating pain.

As soon as I could manage it, I hobbled out to fetch some water and wash my leg. It was very tender, but despite the pain I pressed on my calf to make sure all the pus was out. Then I went back in and lay on the ground with my foot raised so the wound would keep draining. When my mother came back with the other slave laborers that evening, I was a little hopeful. I told her I'd gotten some medical treatment for the wound, and now maybe it would get better.

The women helped my mother gather some fresh weeds to put under me in place of the blood- and pus-soaked straw I'd been sleeping on. For the first night since I'd been wounded—who knows how many days ago—I actually slept peacefully. If not tomorrow, at least the next day I would be able to go back to work, and as long as I could work I would survive.

Morning came. I felt refreshed. My leg still couldn't

support my tiny weight, but I was sure I was going to get better now. After our meager morning meal I tried to encourage my mother as she left for work. Then I limped back and lay down to rest with my foot up, praying that no Kapo would come into the shed and decide to torment me for the fun of it, praying that my mother's strength would hold out, and praying that my wound would heal. I recited all the prayers I remembered from going to synagogue with my father during my early childhood, and I thought about the wonderful man my father had been. Then I dozed off and dreamt about my father. He was in heaven, and a voice said that his merit would save my mother and me. I had other happy dreams. I was living with both of my parents in a paradise called the Land of Israel, a land of milk and honey. I was married to a handsome orange-grower, and we had lots of healthy children. I took them to the beach in the hot sun, and the waves beat on the shore.

I believed in my prayers, but by that evening I could see that they had not been answered. The leg was still infected. In fact, the infection had spread to my upper leg, and it had begun swelling again. My fever returned. Desperate now, my mother asked her friends for medical advice. She herself had learned something about medicine and first aid from her brother Jakob, the physician. No one else there knew anymore than she did, so she decided to go ahead and try her own remedy.

She heated some sand in a tin can on the fire and wrapped the hot sand in a rag. She placed the bag of hot sand on the infection, hoping it would disinfect the wound and draw out the pus. The wound did open, and some of the pus flowed out, but the treatment was as painful as the wound, and the infection remained as strong as ever.

The next day my fever was high, but I was aware enough of my surroundings to be frightened and weep. I knew my leg would never get better now. Either the infection would spread and I would get blood poisoning and die, or else the Kapos would finish me off and throw my body into a ditch before I died from the infection. I was nothing but a useless parasite.

I didn't think of the third possibility, which is actually what happened. One morning three Kapos, including the head of the camp, sauntered into the shed, took a good look at me, and made their decision: *Sie ist hoffnungslos*— she's hopeless. "Tomorrow, we're sending you to the hospital."

That's what they told me, but I didn't think it was true. By the time we were in the labor camp, all the adults knew about the gas chambers and crematoria. I heard them use the word "crematorium." My mother tried to hide the full truth from me. I knew it meant something horrible, I wasn't sure exactly what, and I also wasn't terribly anxious to find out. Still, it was clear that the Nazis were sending me to my death. I was terribly afraid and worried about losing my mother forever. I had lost all hope.

I didn't want to tell my mother. I thought they would take me away while she and the other women were out working. She would come back from work, I wouldn't be there, and she didn't have to know exactly what had happened to me. But I was too weak to bear the idea of parting from my mother forever without even saying goodbye. When she lay down next to me that evening on those putrid-smelling weeds, I said, "Mother, tomorrow they're sending me back to Stutthof." She was too overcome with grief to answer me with words. She lay next to me and sobbed. 'Don't worry," I told her. "They told me they were sending me to the hospital. I'll get better, and then they'll send me back here with you."

We both knew I was lying. She hugged me all night long, and by the morning she had made up her mind. This was when my mother sacrificed herself for me. When the Kapos lined the women up to march to work, my mother burst out in shouts and tears: "Send me to Stutthof with my daughter. I'm sick too. What good am I without her?"

The Kapos didn't care about her. She wasn't a good worker. One "old" woman more or less didn't matter to them. A Kapo was assigned to take us away.

"To the train, march, you sows!" he shouted, as if his shouting could make it happen. The railroad siding was far away, a couple of kilometers, and I couldn't walk at all. I took one step and fell. The Kapo kicked me furiously. "On your feet, you filthy bitch!" My mother helped me up. "Carry her," he shouted at my mother. I put my arm around my mother's shoulders, and she tried to help me along, but she was too weak. We hardly made any progress.

When he realized that my mother wasn't strong enough to carry me to the railroad, he stopped us. The Kapo apparently didn't know exactly what to do with us. He had orders to get us to the train, but no one had told him how he was to do it. What was going to happen?

We halted about twenty or thirty steps beyond the camp fence, a bizarre trio: two filthy figures in ragged, stinking clothes—an emaciated woman in her early forties, who looked as though she were sixty, and an equally emaciated teenage girl, so thin and small she might be ten, with one leg dangling uselessly in the air—and the Kapo, a well-fed young German thug, dressed in a clean, warm uniform, carrying a whip and a gun, and looking at us with cruel indifference. There we stood, in a broad, almost empty field. Except for the guards' quarters, not a house was visible. The world was empty except for the prison camp, and in the distance, across a rutted expanse scoured by the winter winds, wound the railroad tracks. It was a gray, sunless, chilly day, but not too cold for flies to swarm around the pus from my wound. Sometime during the morning a service train would go by, and we would be put on it if we managed to reach the tracks. Otherwise, somewhere between where we now stood and those tracks, we would die.

The Kapo was getting angrier and angrier. In a moment, I knew he was going to shoot us or beat us to death. His arms were twitching with frustration. I imagined our miserable bodies thrown into a ditch to rot, or just left in the field for the stray dogs. My leg hurt me violently, and I was feverish. Perhaps it wouldn't be so bad to be dead, if that meant the end of the pain.

Then we were saved by a friend of ours. A young woman from our camp saw us helpless in the field, I unable to walk and my mother too weak to help me. The young woman volunteered to help drag me to the train. This was one of the most generous gestures someone could possibly make. She couldn't be sure that she herself was strong enough to carry me all that distance. If she faltered, she'd be shot with us. And of course, she had no guarantee that she wouldn't be thrown onto the train to Stutthof with my mother and me when she finally got to the railroad with us. She knew all that, yet when she saw we needed her help, she took the risk. I owe my life to her, and I can't even remember her name.

I kept one arm around my mother's shoulder and put my other around the woman's, and then we started toward the railroad tracks with the Kapo sauntering along behind us, kicking us or whipping us whenever he thought we were moving too slowly. None of us was more than skin stretched tightly across bones, and, as light as I was, the woman and my mother barely had the strength to support me. They dragged me for two kilometers or more. The ground was rough and the walking, hard. We kept stumbling. I don't know how long it took. I hardly remember anything in my life taking so long. Every step hurt all three of us. I could hear them groan and pant as they walked, and I felt sorry for them. But I was in horrible pain, too. It was hard for me to keep my bad leg from banging on the ground, and every time it touched anything, even when a dry weed brushed against it, agonizing flashes of pain shot up my leg and made my body shake. My arms ached, too. It felt as if the woman and my mother were pulling them out of the sockets. I moaned softly. I didn't dare cry out. That might make the Kapo angry, and he'd shoot all three of us.

At last we reached the railroad siding. A guard stood there with a small group of other sick prisoners who had become useless to the Nazis. Their faces were indifferent, not a flicker of response to our arrival, to anything, as if they were dead already, as if they couldn't feel anything anymore. The Kapo left my mother and me with that appalling group and marched the woman who had volunteered to help us back off toward the labor camp. We never saw her again.

The guard let us sit, but some of the sick prisoners were too indifferent to take advantage of that unusual favor. We waited for the train in silence. My arms ached, my leg was throbbing, I was hungry and thirsty, and I felt sad for my mother, who sat next to me with her head down, worn out from the long effort of carrying me. I put my rough hand out and squeezed my mother's hand. She squeezed back, though she didn't have the heart to look at me. At least our souls were still alive.

Finally the train came, a string of cattle cars. The guards threw us into the train and slammed the door. Although we weren't crammed in and suffocating, still we barely had the strength to find comfortable positions. We lay where we had been thrown on filthy straw on the floor of the cattle car. The train kept stopping and starting, waiting for long hours in one place or another. No one brought us food or water, of course.

Sometimes they threw more prisoners into our car. It happened that Hanni, a woman I still know, was one of those prisoners. She had been at another forced labor camp with her mother, and her mother had become too weak to continue working. Now Hanni was being sent back to Stutthof with her. She was appalled to see how the infection on my leg had weakened me, but she tried to comfort my mother. It was a long, slow, painful ride back to the concentration camp at Stutthof.

At last the train slowed and creaked to a stop. Guards rolled open the doors with a crash. Most of the emaciated prisoners on the floor of the car were too weak to say anything or to look up. The guards shouted orders at us: "Out of the train!" Laboriously, Hanni helped us all down, her mother, my mother, and me. My leg hurt so much I couldn't stand without support. Many of the other prisoners didn't have the strength to rise from the floor of the railroad car. Guards climbed into the cattle cars and kicked them down onto the platform. They lay where they had been thrown. I remember staring with horror and helpless pity at those apathetic people, starving and swollen with malnutrition.

In the labor camp we had been isolated, a small group not too closely supervised from above, not run by very well trained or qualified people, and things hadn't always been done with legendary Teutonic efficiency. Now we were on a well-organized assembly line that was to take us inexorably to our deaths.

We were gathered outdoors. A fierce winter wind slashed at us. The Nazi guards, bundled up in warm winter coats lined with fur stolen from us Jews, crossed their arms and stamped their feet to keep warm. We were almost naked, not protected from the cold by even the thinnest layer of fat, but some of the prisoners had become too apathetic even to turn their backs to the wind.

The first stop was called *Entlausung* (delousing). We really did need to be deloused. We were filthy. We stank. Our clothes were alive with fat lice. The lice swarmed over our scalps. Our emaciated flesh was swollen with them. They sucked our blood. One could die from the lice.

If we couldn't walk to the *Entlausung*, they threw us onto a kind of big wagon that they called a *Karre*. Polish criminal prisoners, men who had committed serious, violent crimes, loaded and pulled the wagons. They got much more to eat than the Jews, so they were a lot stronger and healthier than we were. I was too weak even to walk from the railroad platform to the wagons. Hanni and my mother supported me and brought me over there. Then, effortlessly a Polish prisoner picked me up and threw me onto a pile of half-dead, louse-ridden prisoners, all sharp bones. He threw other women on top of me and then set off. My mother walked alongside as he wheeled us to the delousing. Hanni and her mother were separated from us then. Her mother died in the gas chambers at Stutthof, and I didn't see Hanni again until after the liberation.

Someone was lying on top of my infected leg. The pain was phenomenal, and I nearly passed out. From the wagon I couldn't see where they were taking us. I was in too much pain even to think about it. Every jolt jammed some other poor woman's knee into my leg, and I let myself scream in agony. No one told me to stop. I tried to wriggle into a less painful position, but I couldn't. The other women hardly moved. Occasionally I heard a soft groan.

The ride was soon over anyway. The prisoner who was pulling the wagon upended it and dumped us out onto the ground, a tangle of stiff bodies. I pulled myself free and got to my feet despite the pain. We were assembled in an enormous hangar with a dirt floor. This was a scene of tremendous confusion. Those of us who were aware of our surroundings were panic-stricken. Kapos rushed around, cursing and beating people seemingly at random. They forced us into lines and began to process us by having Jewish prisoners cut off our hair. The barbers couldn't look us in the eyes. They knew where we were going. They didn't have the heart to talk to us. Their clippers were dull and they half tore the hair off my head. I watched it fall to the ground. A lethargic prisoner with a broom gathered all the fallen hair into a huge, indistinguishable mass.

At least my mother was still at my side. She was bald too. I looked at her quickly. My eyes glassed over, and I turned away.

After the haircut there was a selection. Some of us were going to be cremated immediately, others would have to wait their turn. At every other selection my mother had been the one in danger, and I was the one who was sure of passing. This time she stood in front of me to try to conceal my disability. She was sent to the right. Then my turn came. Try as I did to appear vigorous and smile cheerfully, the SS doctor saw that I was straining to stand straight on one foot, and he sent me to the left.

My mother had lingered to hear what my fate was to be. When she heard the verdict, she turned around to hug me. We clung to each other and wept. Let them curse us and beat us to death. It didn't matter. We had kept each other alive for so long. We had already lost so much. This was the end for us. I was saying farewell to my mother forever. It was an unbearably painful parting. Each of us felt sorrier for the other than we did for ourselves.

Until that moment I had denied the finality of what was happening to us. But now there was no denying it. We clung to each other while the guards screamed at us. Finally, they rushed forward and pulled us apart. They shoved my mother into the small group of those set aside to be killed later, and they threw me in among the comatose prisoners we called *Mussulmen*, the ones slated for immediate elimination, who had given up hope completely.

We cried out to each other. "Be brave, Mother," I shouted in German. "Try to stay alive."

At that moment a woman in civilian clothes came up to me. Later I found out that she was the camp commander's secretary. She had apparently seen my mother and me while we were parting, and she had heard us talking in German.

"Is that your mother?" she asked me. I said yes. "Horrible," she said, "horrible."

"What can be more horrible than death?" I said.

"No, this is more horrible, more horrible," she answered, rushing away.

I didn't think about her anymore.

Now the Kapos ordered us to strip off our clothes and throw them onto a huge pile. Brutally, they stripped the prisoners, who were too weak to understand or carry out their order. Once my hair, my clothes, and my mother were gone, I was reduced to absolute zero. All I had were my skin and bones and the virulent infection in my leg.

The other prisoners with me, the *Mussulmen*, seemed to be dead already. They had been starved and abused until they were barely conscious. With all their hair shaved off, their heads looked like naked skulls with huge eyes staring out indifferently at their fate.

Everywhere I turned my eyes there were emaciated, naked female bodies, so shriveled from prolonged deprivation that they hardly looked like women any longer—mothers, wives, and daughters, women who had once made love, given birth, and nurtured children, were now reduced to a mockery of humanity. I closed my eyes to avoid seeing that gruesome scene, that vast tangle of bones scarcely covered by skin, the bald heads. Their skin was stretched tight and mottled with bruises, sores, and insect bites. Only their eyes remained human, somehow more than human now, in contrast to everything else. Their eyes asked for pity, crying out, "Just let us die in peace now."

Even with my own eyes closed tight, I couldn't shut out that sight. It penetrated my eyelids even more powerfully than it had when my eyes were open.

I felt nothing but grief and pain: the pain in my leg, the pain in my stomach from months of hunger, and the soreness in my heart at parting from my mother. I crossed my arms, balancing on one leg as best I could.

We were in a large enclosure, and it was warm. I had been cold for so many months that I hardly recognized the feeling of warmth. I could see where the heat was coming from. At the far end of the enclosure were enormous furnaces. Between me and the furnaces stood an apathetic crowd of *Mussulmen*. They were completely finished, with no hope of life anymore. They were to be my last companions on earth. I wasn't comatose, though. I was completely conscious, even though I no longer had any ideas. I could see the criminal prisoners standing at the mouth of the furnaces and throwing the *Mussulmen* into the fire. They were so nearly dead, they couldn't put up any kind of a struggle. The Nazis didn't bother sending them to the gas chambers before cremating them. They had them thrown into the ovens alive, and the *Musselmen* died instantly in the intense heat of the ovens.

More and more victims were being shoved into the room behind me, and I was forced forward, toward the ovens. The only way I could cling to life was by pushing my way backward, away from the furnaces, wiggling between the new arrivals. I did that as long as I could, but my leg hurt too much to keep it up. I could barely stand, and the mass of skeletal, naked bodies kept pushing me forward, no matter how I struggled.

Now I was so close that I could see the faces of the Polish prisoners as they threw live bodies into the fire. They grabbed the women any which way and shoved them in headfirst. Sometimes, if a woman was too tall to fit into the oven, only the top part of her body was burned, and they had to push her feet in after her. It took some time before a body was completely burned up. There were delays, but no one screamed. No one struggled. The victims were indifferent, hundreds of women reduced to absolute apathy by disease and malnutrition, grief and exhaustion, but I was fully conscious, aware of my nakedness, aware of the pain in my leg, aware of the heat of the fierce flames in front of me. Then, when I saw my turn was next, I froze. I became unconscious like the others, like stone. I wouldn't have screamed or struggled when those coarse hands grabbed me. The criminal brutes would have picked me up and thrown me right into the furnace like the other women, and I wouldn't even have been able to make a gesture to remind them that I was a human being.

Then, did I hear the Voice? Was it a dream? At that moment, when I was right in front of the oven, a door opened at the end of the room. There stood the camp commander, a short man of about forty-five, with dark brown hair and a chest covered with medals. His hat glistened with bright insignia. He stood there, rigid, with two stretcher-bearers behind him, and he pointed at me. He shouted, "Take that girl out of here."

Instead of burning me, like the others, the Polish workers put me on the stretcher. The camp commander ordered to have me taken to the *Krankenrevier*, something like a field hospital. There, at the field hospital, Jewish prisoners working as nurses and orderlies cleaned the dirt off my whole body and bandaged my wounded leg. "It will have to be amputated," I heard someone saying. I couldn't understand what was happening. I could only think about my mother. Where was she now?

The German woman who had spoken to me after the selection came in now, carrying a purple nightgown. "Put this on her," she ordered. She looked at me, "I told the camp commander to save you." She turned on her heels and left before I could thank her or ask about my mother.

To this day it is an absolute mystery to me why I was saved. I have puzzled over it ever since. If it weren't for all the others whom they killed, you could say it was a miracle.

What had the secretary seen in me? Was it because my mother and I spoke pure German? Maybe it was because I was one of the only conscious people there—young and relatively healthy-looking, despite my infected leg. How had she been able to convince the camp commander? Perhaps he had a picture of his children on his desk, and the secretary told him I looked like his daughter. What did he have in mind for me? I have only questions, no answers.

The camp commander gave orders to have them operate on my leg. They dressed me like a princess in that purple nightgown and carried me out of the field hospital. At the door stood the camp commander. He put up one hand to halt the stretcher and looked at me with a strange expression. Did he feel pity? His face betrayed no emotion. "I saved you," he said coldly.

"No," I answered. Where did I get the gall, the courage, the confidence or faith? It came to me naturally at that moment, somehow. I looked that vicious murderer in the face and said, "Where is my mother? You took her away from me."

From the Camp Hospital to the Burning Ship

CHAPTER FIVE

The camp commander only asked me Mother's name, and nothing on his face betrayed his reaction.

He wheeled about and strutted back to his office, but he must have given someone an order to find my mother. A Kapo wrote the name on a slip of paper and apparently went out to look for her. I remembered the day we had first been transported to Stutthof from the Kovno ghetto, how I had run from one woman to another to find my mother, and how I had only come upon her by chance. I, her own daughter, hadn't been able to pick her out of that vast crowd of dejected women. The Kapo didn't know her and certainly didn't care whether he found her or not. Would he take the trouble to pick her out? What did he have to go by? Names meant nothing in a concentration camp. But I imagine he must have known approximately where mother had been sent, because he knew what time we had arrived. How, I wondered, could he find anyone in that immense, anonymous mass of shaven women, who were waiting in barracks until their turn came to be killed?

My leg still hurt me terribly, but at least I was clean now, and dressed more warmly. The soft, purple nightgown was a welcome change after the filthy clothes I'd worked in and slept in for months at the labor camp in Torun, and even more so after the humiliation of being stripped naked here in Stutthof.

The two orderlies bore me along on the stretcher like a kind of princess in a grotesque fairy tale. Masses of miserable women were gathered outside, condemned to cruel death. Somewhere, among all those doomed souls, was my mother. I was very worried about her. The last time she was separated from me, she had tried to strangle herself. What would she do now?

Luckily she wasn't all alone. She had been thrown in among some women who had known her in the Kovno ghetto. They sat together under some bare trees on the cold ground and tried to comfort each other. The other women were familiar with the procedures at Stutthof, and deeply familiar with grief as well. They told mother, "Trudi isn't alive any longer. No one ever returns from the ovens. You must take comfort in the thought that at least she can't suffer anymore. But you must try to live, for the sake of her memory." Those who survived always gave each other reasons to survive.

At that moment my stretcher was carried through the enclosure where my mother was sitting. Everyone was looking in my direction. She saw me, but she didn't recognize me. How could she? She had last seen me filthy and weak, hobbling among a group of *Mussulmen* who were about to be thrown into the flames, and now I was clean, reclining on a stretcher, and dressed in a soft, warm, purple nightgown. It was inconceivable that her daughter, who, she had just been told, was surely dead, could now appear, borne along like some kind of princess in the midst of the horror of the concentration camp. It didn't register that I was truly her daughter. For her this was more like some kind of wish-fulfillment dream than reality. No one had ever been saved from the crematorium. But there I was, not only alive, but also protected by the camp commander.

I recognized my mother and called out, "Mama! It's me!" The stretcher-bearers halted.

My mother heard me and cried out in disbelief, "Trudi, are you alive?" This was like a dream. The thing she most wanted in the world was actually happening, I was being brought back to her, and she couldn't believe it.

From the stretcher I called back to her, "Yes, they didn't kill me." She stood up and tried to push her way toward me through the crowd, despite her frailty. I reached my hand out toward her. Our hands touched, and our hearts were joined again.

The Kapo who had been looking for my mother pointed his finger at her and shouted an order: "Bring that woman into the hospital!" So my mother followed the stretcher. Suddenly there was again a chance that we both might live.

The Kapos set my stretcher down in the hospital and relayed the camp commander's orders: They were to operate on my leg. The medical staff of the hospital were Lithuanian Jews. The doctor who treated my wound was a woman whose last name was Kaplan. She had been among the best surgeons in Kovno, and she knew my uncle Jakob and my mother's family. She recognized us.

She examined the wound and told us that the simplest thing would be to amputate below the knee, but that she thought she could save my leg. At that point I still expected to die of the infection and didn't see why she was making such a fuss about saving the leg. I just nodded blankly.

The doctor did the best she could, with the limited

supplies and equipment available in the concentration camp hospital, the Krankenrevier. The facility for the Jews was separate from the one that treated the Gentile prisoners. In no sense was it like a real hospital. It was unsanitary, uncomfortable, unheated, and vastly overcrowded.

There was no anesthetic, just something to dull the pain very slightly. Dr. Kaplan cut away the blighted flesh, and every stroke of her scalpel was agony. We both gritted our teeth: I to keep from screaming, and she to keep working calmly despite the pain she was causing me. Finally she had cleaned and disinfected the wound as well as she could, and she gave orders to have me sent me back to the ward where we slept.

At least a day passed before I was strong enough to take stock of my surroundings. Like all the patients, my mother and I slept on a wooden platform—*Britsche* is what we called it. We regarded ourselves as very fortunate. Usually they made four prisoners share each of these bed-platforms, but as a mark of our favored status, they let my mother and me have one to ourselves. Of course no one had any sheets, though there were some filthy old army blankets, and we all got the standard starvation rations: watery potato-peel soup with grains of dirt in it and some hard bread. Unlike the labor camp, where I was too exhausted to be open to anyone except my mother, in the Krankenrevier, despite our suffering, I made friends with some of the other patients.

After my mother and I had been lying in the hospital for only a few days, the camp commander entered the room and rushed right to our shelf. With an iron-hard, flat, cruel voice, he commanded me, "Get up and go into the office! That is my order!"

To my mother he shouted, "Get up! Start mopping the floor here!" He pointed to the corridor. As fast as she could, my mother got off the wooden shelf, and he saw that she was dressed in filthy rags. He ordered a Kapo, "Bring them work clothes, right away."

I still hadn't gotten up. He looked at me again and screamed, "Out of there!"

"I can't walk," I protested. The only time I had gotten up at all was to go to the latrines, and I had only managed with my mother helping me at every step. It was dreadfully painful.

"Out of bed!" he shouted, and I had to obey, despite the pain. I couldn't imagine what he wanted from me.

He looked down at my feet. I had one wooden clog on my good foot. He gave another order to the Kapos: "Bring her a pair of shoes!" He left the room.

In a very short time the Kapos came back with slightly better clothes for my mother and me, and a pair of used army boots. We put on the clothes as fast as we could. Pulling that heavy, stiff boot over my wounded leg was torture, but I knew I had to do it. The camp commander came strutting back and yelled, "Why aren't you in the office?"

"I can't walk!"

"You must."

There was no argument with that command. I scrambled into the hospital office as fast as I could, despite the terrible pain, hopping on my good foot.

The camp commander followed me. He made me sit at a table and handed me a list of names: "Copy that list. If anyone asks what you're doing, say, 'office work.'" The list contained the names of prisoners who had died in the last day. It was very long. Outside the window I could see the corpses piled up. I recognized some of the friends I had made in the Krankenrevier.

I soon found out why the camp director had sent my mother and me out to work. A delegation of very high-ranking SS officers had arrived at Stutthof on an inspection tour. Within minutes, the officers arrived at the hospital with evil in their eyes. They were among the most savage murderers in the German army, dressed in immaculate uniforms, gaudy with battle ribbons and medals, and sinister with their daggers and swagger-sticks and shiny black leather belts and boots.

In the hospital barrack the Nazi officers staged a small, private selection for their own amusement. They made the sick women take off their clothes and prance back and forth, naked, in front of them, like models in a fashion show. They looked them over carefully, making nasty little jokes to each other, and they decided which ones were fit for work or sexual abuse. They enjoyed seeing the women's embarrassment, and when someone was too skinny and frail for their taste, they got pleasure from pronouncing the dread words: "*ins Krematorium!*" (to the Crematorium!).

They noticed my mother out in the hall with a bucket and mop, cleaning the floor as if that were her regular job (she had had a lot of practice at that in the military hospital in the Kovno ghetto), and they ignored her. They also ignored me, the office worker. I couldn't see what was going on in the ward and was only told about it afterward.

My mother scrubbed away at the floor while the officers were parading the naked women up and down, and her heart ached for the women. A lot of them were removed from the hospital to be gassed during that selection.

When the SS officers left, my mother and I were told to return to the ward. The Kapos took back our work clothes. The camp rule was that a woman could stay in the hospital for seven days. If she recovered, she was sent out to a labor camp again. If she didn't, she was gassed. Without the camp commander's protection I would have been sent to the gas chamber. They kept culling the ranks of the sick women, but we were never inspected by senior officers again, and the commander was able to make sure my mother and I weren't taken away without having to disguise us as workers.

The first operation on my infected leg was only partially successful, so they had to open the wound and drain the pus again. I don't know how I lived through that searing pain. My leg was useless and bent, and for a long time, even after the war, I couldn't straighten it completely.

In addition to the weekly selections, low-ranking officers sometimes came to make a surprise inspection. Some of the girls in the hospital were strong enough to stand, and they used to keep watch. When they heard the officers coming, they called out, "*Sechs!*" (Six!). The officers strutted in, solid and well fed, clean and warmly dressed, arrogant and nasty. They passed from wooden shelf to wooden shelf, picking up the blankets with their swagger sticks to look at our bodies. We all tried to smile and look cheerful, to prove we were all right. If they felt like it, they might send anyone they pleased to the gas chambers.

Sometimes I wonder why they bothered to have any kind of hospital for the sick people. The whole point of the concentration camp was to kill Jews, so why do anything to keep them alive? I'm convinced it was because they wanted us to suffer as much as possible. They didn't only want us dead, they wanted to torture us, to break us. You could see in their faces that they enjoyed seeing us in pain. They did everything they could to make things as painful as possible for us. That's why they half starved us, to keep us going as long as possible before we collapsed from hunger.

I don't want anyone to forget the pure cruelty of the camps. They weren't just impersonal death factories, where people were processed in gas chambers and crematoria like some kind of macabre product. They were places where sadistic, bestial criminals were able to carry out their cruelest and most grotesque fantasies on innocent victims. If an epidemic added to our suffering, so much the better, from their point of view, but they kept up some semblance of a hospital and medical care to make our suffering even worse, to remind us of what a human being normally has the right to expect.

Occasionally, a Kapo would come into the hospital barrack and have sex with one of the women, shamelessly, in front of everyone. I remember seeing that and not quite understanding what he was doing to her. I did notice that they had a nicer blanket on their sleeping shelf. The girl probably got a sandwich or a bit of sausage for her sexual favors. We were so hungry all the time that to get any extra food was like finding a huge treasure. But she obviously had no choice anyway. If she hadn't cooperated, she'd have been killed. I also remember that one of the women in the hospital barracks had a baby, but the Kapos took it away and killed it.

My mother and I spoke with each other for hours while we lay together on the wooden sleeping platform in the hospital barrack. We remembered the past, the happy times in Frankfurt before the Nazis came to power, and we remembered the wonderful people who were lost: my dear father, my uncle Benno. We wondered whether the Russians had reached the Kovno ghetto in time to save my mother's parents and her brother Jakob. And my mother was deeply worried about my brother Manfred, whom we hadn't seen since the Nazis put us on the trains to Stutthof. Where had they taken him? Was he managing to survive? Would we ever see him again?

I always did my best to imagine a happy future for us. I made up a joyous country that I called the Land of Israel, where we would live in comfort and safety. I imagined all the food we would eat there, luscious fruit and tasty rolls and butter. More than anything, I was possessed by the desire to drink a cup of hot chocolate.

In the hospital we made friends with some of the other women. There was almost nothing to eat, but at least we didn't have to work like slaves and dig trenches in the frozen earth. The days were full of dreadful tension because we never knew when we might be singled out and sent to our deaths. But rumors reached us that the Germans were definitely losing the war, and that was encouraging. We kept wondering when someone would come to save us, and why it was taking so long.

The camp commander used to come once or twice a day and look in on me through a glass window in the door. He never entered the room again, and he didn't talk to me. He just looked at me. Apparently he wanted to see if I was still alive. This, of course, was before the typhus epidemic.

Typhus doesn't really have a cure: either you get better or you die. It's spread by lice, and people who are hungry and weak are especially susceptible to it. A concentration camp is an ideal environment for a typhus epidemic. People were dying from it all the time. Once it broke out, the Germans put everyone who caught the disease in a separate room, and they stayed away.

———

Time passed, and my leg was beginning to get better, but it was still too weak to support me. Meanwhile, things were changing in the camp. After January 1945 they stopped using the gas chamber. If we didn't die by ourselves, the Nazis weren't going to process us in their death factory anymore. Of course, we were all so weak, hungry, and ill that many of us died every day without the help of poison gas. The gas chamber may have been retired, but the crematorium worked overtime.

People around my mother and me were dying by the score every day. First they became *Mussulmen*. Their arms and legs got very thin, but their abdomens swelled up. What haunts my memory most is their glassy eyes. The doctors who took care of us were Jewish slaves like us. They did what they could. There was little or no medicine or equipment, no sanitary bandages or bedding, and no disinfectants. The Jewish staff was supervised closely by Germans. Regardless of the shortage of supplies, they weren't allowed to give us decent treatment anyway. If they tried too hard, they would get into trouble with the authorities. Essentially, there was no care for the sick. A very few lucky ones lived, and the vast majority languished and died.

By early 1945 the Russians started to shell the camp sporadically. The camp commander disappeared. I'll never know what fate he had in mind for me. I heard he ran away, and I don't know whether he was captured and brought to trial after the war. I hope so. I hope he was executed for his crimes. He should have been hanged a hundred times. I would certainly have testified against him if I could. Some quirk in his evil nature led him to save my mother and me, but he was responsible for tens of thousands of murders, and his one act of mercy just makes those other horrible crimes more monstrous.

The first evacuations from Stutthof took place in late January. During the last months of the war, the Nazi concentration camp empire started falling apart. Apparently they wanted to destroy the evidence. In long columns they marched off all the prisoners who were able to walk, about twenty-five thousand people. These were the infamous death marches. Many of the prisoners were shot for faltering on the way to other concentration camps in Germany, where the Nazis were taking them, and others died of exhaustion, starvation, and exposure to the severe winter cold and wind. Of those who survived the march, many were killed when they reached their destinations.

About ten thousand inmates, including my mother and me, were left in Stutthof; the ones who were too sick or weak to leave on foot. At that time my mother came down with typhus. They brought her to a different section of the hospital barrack, a room with thirty other women who had typhus. It was separate, but it wasn't really quarantined. None of the Germans cared if we went in, caught typhus, and spread it to all the other Jews.

The hospital barrack had a long hallway, with big rooms on both sides. Sick women also lay in the corridors. There were about a hundred patients at any one time, but always different ones. When my mother was moved to the typhus ward, I was placed out in the hallway where there were six wooden platforms, three on each side, with two patients in each platform. I had to share my sleeping platform with a strange woman for the first time since my mother and I had been transported from the Kovno ghetto.

People were dying of typhus at a tremendous rate. The camp fell into disarray. The crematorium couldn't cope with the volume of corpses, so they built a huge pyre to take care of the excess. Thick smoke and the smell of burning bodies filled the air night and day. Meanwhile, the Russians continued to shell the camp from time to time, but they didn't come.

I spent the days lying on a shelf in the old hospital barrack. The inspections and selections had stopped, and the Germans left us more or less alone. In the disorder I was able to hobble over to the quarantine section to find out how my mother was. It still hurt me terribly to move my leg, but I missed my mother too much to stay away. Usually I made those visits later in the day, after we got our ration of soup, because no patient ever left her place before the soup was distributed. We used to wait on the platforms for our bowl of thin soup as if it were a gift from heaven. If you missed it you wouldn't get a second chance, and that was all the food there was.

One morning I snapped wide awake, as if a nail had been driven into my thigh. I was filled with anxiety about my mother. A voice, sometimes I think it was the voice of God, shouted in my head, "You must get over to the quarantine section to find out how she is!"

Even though I might miss my soup, the voice was so strong that I had to obey it. My leg hurt the most in the cold mornings, but I couldn't let the pain stop me. I got out of bed and limped over to the quarantine section as fast as I could. I was afraid my mother might be dead. I rushed to her sleeping platform. She noticed I was there, and I asked her, "Did you sleep well last night?"

Very feebly she answered, "Yes, thank God." What a relief! She wasn't delirious with fever. Perhaps she would survive.

Just at that moment a Russian shell landed on the hospital barrack. Just the noise of the explosion knocked me down. When I had pulled myself to my feet again, I saw there was blood beneath my mother's bed. We both felt our bodies to see whether we were wounded. No, we were intact. Then we saw that shrapnel had ripped through the walls and killed some of the people in the beds at the end of the room. People were screaming in pain and fright. Smoke was coming from the corridor where I had just been lying. I hopped back to my place, but it was gone. The shell had fallen right there, and all my friends were dead. Everyone in the room had been ripped to shreds by shrapnel.

Incredibly, my mother recovered from typhus. I don't understand how she managed. Once the fever left her she nearly starved to death. There was no extra food in the camp, and it's well known that after this disease people get fantastically hungry. You're so ravenous you go crazy. You want to eat everything: dirt, the earth, grass, plants, weeds—whatever you can put into your mouth. As much as the typhus patients needed it, no one even tried to obtain more to eat for them than that thin soup, not even extra drinking water. There were no doctors anymore.

After marching off most of the prisoners in late January 1945, the highest officers among the Germans also abandoned the camp, and we remained with a lot fewer guards. Of course, there was no possibility of escaping or rebelling. We were all too sick to walk more than a few steps; otherwise we would have been sent away with the other prisoners. The Kapos didn't behave quite as savagely as before. There was less torture and indiscriminate killing. We knew the Red Army was on its way. We could sense that something momentous was afoot, but no one made any move to rescue us. We asked, Where was the world? How could human beings let these crimes take place?

As the Russians approached the camp seemed about to lapse into confusion. We still got some food every day, but we never knew when it would be coming. Finally, in late April, they began the final evacuation from the Stutthof concentration camp. Weak as we were, they made us trudge along the seacoast on foot, without giving us any food. It was a six-hour march. We were surrounded by panic and disorder. The guards kept shouting, *"Schnell! Schnell!"* (Fast! Fast!). My bad leg suffered terribly on the march. It could barely support my tiny weight, but I had to walk by myself. I bit my lip and kept on. Mother was too weak from typhus to help me. Actually, I was afraid she would die any minute. Redemption would surely come, but we might give up the ghost first.

They marched us along the Baltic seacoast. A brisk wind blew in off the water and chilled us to the bone. At last we got to the three big cattle barges they had prepared for us. After some waiting around and confusion, the guards loaded us onto the barges. They were good-sized boats with large, deep holds and no railing around the narrow deck. A metal ladder led down into the hold. They sent about a hundred women down that ladder, making us lie down in filthy straw.

The barges put out to sea, and we had no idea where they were headed. All we heard was the roar of the engines and the pounding of waves against the sides. When it rained, the rain poured down on us and wet the straw. When the water was rough, the barges rolled so wildly we were sure they would capsize. Many of the women were seasick, and we were all petrified. We lay on that damp, filthy straw and stared up at the hatch cover, day and night, praying only that the war would be over before we died.

Women kept dying. They gave us no food, not even drinking water. We had to drink the filthy liquid, rain mixed with seawater, that lay on the bottom of the hold beneath the straw. We chewed on the straw like animals,

151

just to fool our stomachs. German crewmen leaned over the hatch opening and jeered at us every once in a while: "You cows! You pigs! Let's see you die like swine!"

Aside from the Germans who were running the boat, there were Polish and Ukrainian prisoners down in the hold with us, the criminals who had done all the manual labor at Stutthof. Among ourselves we called them cavemen. They were barbaric, and we were petrified of them. Their main job was to throw our corpses into the sea.

I've often wondered why the Germans didn't just throw everyone overboard right away, since they planned to kill us anyway. Again, I think it's because they wanted to make us suffer as horribly as possible until the very end. Often, however, they didn't wait until a woman was dead. They threw a few of the older women and the ones who got very sick into the water just to be rid of them. I was afraid they would notice my mother and throw her overboard, too, so I lay on top of her and hid her in the straw beneath me. That also kept us warm.

The German crew didn't have any fresh food for themselves, but they had bread in tins. Sometimes, on a whim, one of them would give some to us. Once a crewman singled me out and threw a small tin of bread, only 150 grams, into the hold for me. The other women saw it and scurried over to try and grab it away from me, but the crewman said, "It's for the girl." I clung fiercely to the can and managed to keep it, but I had no way of opening it. I groped under the straw until I found a nail and tried to use that to open it. I was so hungry I didn't care whether I cut my hands on the can, just as long as I got a bit of bread for my mother and myself.

I tried to keep the can out of sight while I struggled to open it, but the other women kept their eyes on me. When I got it open they fell upon me and almost killed me to take the bread away from me. I managed to take some out for myself and my mother before the other women grabbed the can out of my hands. We were so hungry, we behaved like wild animals. We would have murdered each other for food.

Time went by and things got worse. I don't know where our barges were trying to sail. By early May, most of the Baltic coast was in Allied hands (though we women down in the hold had no way of knowing that). We heard the heavy roar of British bombers in the air, unopposed by the high-pitched motors of Luftwaffe fighters. That was a clear sign that the end of the war was in sight.

The voyage dragged on for ten days. Then on May 4, nearly the last day of the war, a British bomb exploded near our barge and damaged it. Luckily it wasn't a direct hit, but a fire started somewhere on board. The barge sprang a leak and the stern began to sink. All of us were in a panic, but hardly any of us had the strength to move.

I reacted first, instinctively, like a horse in a burning barn. I jumped to my feet and forced my mother to get up, too. Then I leaped over to the iron ladder. I was the first to reach it. My mother followed close behind me. The ladder was hot in my hands. I quickly climbed up to the narrow deck and then turned around to pull my mother up after me. The other prisoners, including the Polish and Ukrainian criminals, had roused themselves by now. They swarmed around the ladder. Seized by hysterical fear, they grabbed at my mother's feet as I pulled on her arms.

153

Luckily she was wearing wooden clogs, *Klumpes*, and they came off in the other prisoners' hands. I pulled my mother up the ladder, and the two of us ran toward the highest place on the deck, right near the edge.

For the first time I had a chance to look out at the sea. It took my eyes some time to get used to the strong light and broad horizon. It was a brisk, clear day. A few other ships and barges full of prisoners were in sight. Some of them seemed to have been hit by shells as well. British warships were also visible, approaching us. The German vessels had hoisted white flags. They were surrendering. These were flags of peace. I hugged my mother. The war was over. We were still alive.

Meanwhile, however, our barge was burning and sinking. More and more of the surviving prisoners from Stutthof kept emerging up the hot metal ladder from the hold. They were crowded on the narrow deck now, struggling toward the high side of the listing ship. What a sight we were, ragged, emaciated women, weighing almost nothing.

For some reason the German cook was in charge, giving orders to everyone. There were hardly any other Germans left on the barge. I don't know what happened to them all. The cook stood on the edge of the deck, not far from me, and tried to keep order. He was wrapped in a blanket, and there was something very odd about it. A dark red stain was spreading rapidly across it. I was puzzled by that stain until I realized the cook was wounded. Drops of blood spattered the deck at his feet.

He looked around in panic, trying to think of something to do to save the sinking barge. Suddenly he screamed, *"Das Schiff ist zu schwer!"* (The ship is too heavy!). *"Die Juden ins Wasser!"* (Jews in the water!). He wanted to lighten the load. For a moment, nobody moved. I looked around the deck and saw all sorts of heavy things they could throw overboard: big crates of ammunition, machinery, even a bicycle. Why the Jews?

He shouted again, hysterically, *"Die Juden ins Wasser!!"* The Polish and Ukrainian prisoners began to move forward to obey his orders. They started pushing us toward the edge of the deck. This was impossible. It must be an error. The British navy was within sight, the Germans had hoisted white flags, and yet they were throwing us into the icy sea! Had we survived everything only for this? All thirty of the remaining women, taken together, probably didn't weigh enough to make any difference on that sinking barge.

Things happened very slowly. A British vessel was drawing closer, but that didn't stop the Polish and Ukrainian prisoners from pushing us toward the edge of the deck. There was no railing. We would fall in, one by one, if no one stopped them. As much as they could, the women pushed back, but they were so light and frail they couldn't do anything. I was the one closest to the water, because I had been the first one out of the hold. Now I stood at very edge of the deck, leaning back against the women behind me so I wouldn't fall in the sea. I looked down and saw the clear, freezing water. If I fell in, it would be my death. The wind blew in my face. The British ship steamed toward us, going so slowly that it seemed it would never reach us.

From where did the strength and inspiration come to

me then? I remembered my father's stories of martyrs dying with the words *Shema Yisrael* on their lips ("Hear, O Israel" [the Lord our God, the Lord is One]). I was not going to die without crying out once more to God. He had let terrible tragedies happen. He had seemed absent for years. But perhaps He might hear me at this final moment. I raised my hands in a dramatic gesture and shouted as loudly as I could, "Hear, O Israel!" But I meant, "Hear me, God!" I was only a little girl, reduced to skin and bones. Where did I get the strength to shout?

I needed every ounce of that strength to keep from being pushed into the water. I resisted the pressure from behind, but it was hopeless. I felt myself being pushed over the edge of the deck. I pushed back as best I could, despite my bad leg. In just a moment I would be flung over the edge, plunging down into the sea. It was just waiting for me. I could feel the cold spray on my face. My arms were still raised over my head and I was leaning back on the women behind me. At the same time, I held the last syllable of the prayer as long as I could, remembering the story my father had told me about Rabbi Akiba, who had been tortured to death by the Romans and who shouted the *Shema* in just that way as his soul had left his body.

"What's that!"

Suddenly the German cook who was giving orders stopped everything. "What are you shouting?"

"I'm praying to my God!" I answered proudly.

"You can forget about your God. In a moment you'll be down in the cold water, and the fish will eat you."

"No, they won't," I screamed at him defiantly in German. "God has saved me until now, and He is not going to let me die at the last minute. You Germans will go in the freezing water, not us Jews." I pointed down at the water. "You've lost the war, don't you know? Now the British are coming to get you." I pointed out toward the British warship that was heading toward us, close enough now that we could see the sailors on deck.

Something convinced him to relent. He called out, "*Die Juden bleiben hier!*" (The Jews stay here!). He ordered the Polish and Ukrainian prisoners to stop pushing us, and so none of the thirty surviving women was thrown into the water. My prayer and my self-confidence had stopped him short, and now he had changed his mind.

Perhaps it was his own state of mind. He could feel he was dying of his wound. Whatever it was, he decided to wait until the British came. We fell back, away from the edge of the deck. I looked down at the clear waves again. They were so clean and beautiful, and so full of death. I still hardly believed I wasn't going to be thrown down into the sea.

The cook was standing close to me at the edge of the deck. "Girl," he said to me. I looked him in the eyes. "You impressed me," he went on. He removed his blood-stained blanket and handed it to me. "Warm yourself," he said.

Until that moment I hadn't realized how cold I was. My mother and I huddled together under the bloody blanket, and the cook fainted from loss of blood.

Liberation

CHAPTER SIX

A grotesque band of people stood on the tilting deck of the sinking, burning barge on that early May afternoon in 1945, shivering in the chill as the evening approached: eight German crewmen, some of whom were wounded; four Polish and Ukrainian thugs; and about thirty Jewish women, nightmarishly thin and exhausted. The British warship approached warily, training its guns on us, perhaps expecting a sinister German trick masked by the white flags of surrender.

At last, the British ship drew alongside, towering above us. Over a loudspeaker, in English-accented German, they ordered us all to raise our hands. A sailor cast a heavy line down to our barge, and the interpreter ordered one of the sailors on board to make it fast. Soon they rigged up a rope ladder, and we had to climb up. This was very difficult for us. The distance between the two vessels was considerable, but the knowledge that the Germans had finally lost the war gave us the energy to make it. Besides, if we didn't manage, who would help us?

Everything happened very calmly. The English sailors worked fast and efficiently. They helped us with a will, but there were no smiles on their faces. Perhaps it's hard to smile at people who look the way we did.

They didn't separate the Jews and the Germans on the ship. Suddenly we were clustered with our enemies and former masters, waiting for mugs of hot English tea with sugar and milk. As weak and exhausted as we were, we started fighting with each other to get served first. We had been so degraded by our treatment that we could no longer act like civilized human beings.

The British sailors brought the German cook on board, but he soon died from loss of blood and they buried him unceremoniously at sea. So, despite his orders, it was he, not the few remaining Jews on his barge, who ended up in the cold water. I never returned his blanket to him. I still own it, a symbol of one prayer that was answered.

The British sailors felt sorry for us and wanted to give us piles of food, but the ship's doctor stopped them. He ordered them to give us small portions of soup and bread, saving us from our wild hunger and their goodwill. It had been so long since we had eaten decent food in normal quantities that we could easily have killed ourselves by overeating.

Night had fallen by the time they took us ashore at Kiel and brought us to a school dormitory. There was no controlling the youngest of us. We had feverish energy. Some of us immediately went downstairs, broke into the kitchen, and started gobbling up everything we could. I remember finding some baking soda in a cabinet and being tempted to spoon that into my mouth. Fortunately, I resisted that temptation.

For many of us, including my mother, the sudden abundance of food brought on severe digestive disorders and diarrhea. We hadn't been killed by starvation, but we might die from eating. Looking back on it, I see that during the first weeks of May, the British didn't have any clear idea of what to do with us or how to treat us. They sent us to a hospital staffed by Germans who behaved very badly toward us. They still hated us and tried to humiliate us as though we were prisoners, guilty of some crime. But we weren't at their absolute mercy anymore. We could shout back at them, and we did. That was the first sign that we had begun to acknowledge the fact of our liberation.

Once the fighting was completely over, the British were no longer preoccupied with winning the war. Gradually, as it became clearer to them just who we were and what we had undergone, our treatment improved.

I had dreamt of hot chocolate for years, ever since being shut in the Kovno ghetto. Now, after the liberation, I was offered cocoa, but I couldn't drink it. My digestive system was too delicate, like a baby's. All of us became obsessed with bread. We couldn't get enough of it. We would stuff ourselves with bread and then fill our pockets, so we'd never be without. Even today, when I go through periods of stress, my first thought is: Make sure there's enough bread.

When we climbed up that rope ladder from the sinking German cattle barge to the British warship, we made a momentous transition from the status of slaves or less than slaves to that of human beings who deserved care and medical treatment. We experienced a sudden restoration of the most basic human rights that had been taken away from us, equally suddenly, by the Nazis in 1941. We had been at everyone's mercy, fair game to any "Aryan" who felt like hurting us, exploiting us, humiliating us, or killing us. Suddenly we had human status again. But it took us many months, even years, before we fully assimilated that return to the world of common humanity.

The period in my life from the beginning of the Holocaust to my liberation in 1945 seems removed from the normal stream of time. I had been a young girl in the summer of 1941, when they confined the Jews of Kovno in the ghetto, and I feel as though I remained exactly the same age until 1945, when I was released. When I think of all the time I suffered in the ghetto, in the labor camp, and in the concentration camp, I still think of myself as the small girl who first crossed the narrow bridge into the ghetto with her family, clutching a few precious belongings. Physically, I hardly grew at all during those four years of dreadful hardship. When I was liberated I suddenly began to grow again. I was restored to real time.

Emotionally, too, I had been warped, stunted, and numbed by constant fear, grief, and my desperate desire to survive. Although I used to force myself to smile at the German soldiers during the war in order to beg a piece of bread from them, I hadn't smiled spontaneously, from simple happiness, for years. And I was still only a child. Perhaps the only normal emotion I retained throughout that period was my love for my mother.

A lot of people lost contact with their true personalities because of Nazi cruelty. We weren't human beings any longer. It's only natural for people to behave abnormally during and after what we had experienced. It would be abnormal to be normal after the Holocaust. In fact, it's a miracle that any survivors have been able to resume regular lives, marry, raise families, and live as productive citizens.

I should be like someone made of stone. That's what happened to me at the mouth of the ovens. Like a statue. I lost my wits. I was no longer living. I ought to have stayed that way, I think. That's the only reasonable response to what I went through.

Right after the liberation we lived in a world without laws. We couldn't acclimate to regular life. And we were constantly haunted by that frantic desire for bread. Our bodies began to look strange. They bulged in some places and stayed skinny in others. People used to point us out as concentration camp survivors in the street, but we also used to shout insults at the Germans.

We had to start over again from the beginning, because we didn't have anything left over to continue. At our first medical examination they discovered that my mother and I both had tuberculosis. They put us in a hospital for a month for treatment. Meanwhile, mother's life was in danger. From the very first meals they had given her she had developed diarrhea, and it wouldn't stop. She was dehydrating. She wasn't gaining weight, and it didn't seem as if she had strength to recover. I saw her fading away before my very eyes, and I couldn't stand the sight. Had I saved her and she saved me for this? It couldn't be!

I left the hospital and went to a park. I remember the mild, sunny June weather. Sobbing, I walked among the flowers and trees. I was free, but my freedom meant nothing to me if my mother couldn't live to share it. In the sad conversations we had whispered to each other on our wooden sleeping shelf in Stutthof, my mother and I had shared the dream of taking a walk together in the woods, free of fear, able to relax and enjoy the fresh air, the play of sunshine and shadow through the leaves. That was one of the first things we would do after the war. Now I was in a beautiful forest park, but my mother was too ill to leave her bed and share the beauty of nature with me.

Finally I got to a place where I was all alone, and then I shouted to God, "Give me back my mother!" How did I dare ask for special favors, after what had happened to so many other Jews? What made me think that God would listen to me? I don't know, but something in me made me cry out, desperate not to be left all alone in the world, and, miraculously, that day my mother began to recover. Soon she was able to digest food normally and start off on the long path toward recovery.

We stayed in Kiel for a month or two while we received the urgent medical treatment we needed immediately after the liberation. We received some normal clothing, but we didn't care about clothes at all. We just cared about being free, about walking wherever we wanted to.

We were on our own. There were no social workers or psychologists. The main activity preoccupying everyone was the search for relatives and friends, trying to find out who had survived. Our conversations were a desperate version of what people call "Jewish geography" today: "Where are you from? Where were you during the war? Did you know this person? When did you last see that person? Do you know any of the other people who were with him?" So often we had to give and receive the sad news: "Yes, we knew him." He died here, or he was shot there, or he was gassed somewhere else. The desperate hopes that had sustained people during the war continued to die after the liberation.

We didn't have any real plans for the future. It was clear we would leave Germany. We planned to go to the United States, but we hadn't done anything about it. We had no demands yet. For a while it was easiest just to drift along.

My mother and I still hoped that perhaps her brother Jakob and their parents had survived by hiding in the bunker under the burning Kovno ghetto until the Russians liberated the place, and we had no idea what had become of my brother, Manfred. One of the first things the Jewish relief agencies did was to gather the survivors' names and publish lists. People went through them frantically. It was such a tragic situation. You wanted to stare at the people as they leafed through the lists, so that you could share their hope with them. But at the same time you had to look away, out of respect for their privacy, and also because you knew that the chances of their finding the names they were looking for were small. When it was your own turn, you wanted to be alone. Our faces would be tense with mixed hope and fear. If we found a name, we would be jubilant, but when we failed to find one, we would lapse into depression. We were all so vulnerable, it was pathetic.

Every time a new list came out my mother and I checked for our relatives' names. Miraculously, we saw that someone named Manfred Simon was listed as living in Frankfurt, our native city. It had to be my brother! We decided to go to Frankfurt immediately. We couldn't send a letter to announce our arrival. We didn't have Manfred's exact address, and besides, Germany was in a shambles at the time. The postal service was irregular and untrustworthy. Who could tell when a letter might arrive?

My mother's joyous anticipation of being reunited with

her son was tempered by apprehension: perhaps the report was erroneous. Mother didn't let her hopes get too high. Perhaps it was a different Manfred Simon, or perhaps someone else, for reasons known only to himself, was using the name Manfred Simon. As for me, I had no doubt. I was confident that it was my brother, and I couldn't wait to see him again after more than a year of anxious, fearful separation, when there had been no way of knowing whether any of us would survive.

The trip from Kiel to Frankfurt brought our grief back to life. It revived memories of what my mother had once had, long ago in Frankfurt, and of what she had lost. If only my father had lived to make the trip with her!

Fortunately, the Manfred Simon who was reported to be living in Frankfurt actually was my brother Manfred, and it was fairly easy to find him there, because Dita, his wife, was working for the Jewish Agency. My mother's reunion with her only son was extraordinarily moving. She hugged him and hugged him forever, and I stood next to them and hugged them both.

After the first moment of elation, the three of us stared at each other as though we were ghosts. We had never expected to see each other alive again. A strong memory of Manfred as a little boy flooded my mind. I saw him, my much admired big brother, proud, well dressed, and well groomed. Suffering under the Nazis had changed him almost beyond recognition. He looked much older and more intense than I remembered and imagined him.

I wonder what I looked like to him? I was no longer the skinny little girl he had known in the ghetto. I wasn't a skeleton any longer. I was becoming a young woman now.

Physically, at least, I had begun to recover from the camps. A lot of my hair had grown back, and I had filled out, though my body was all lumpy, fat in some places and bony in others.

When we were liberated, it had been four years since I'd had a mirror. Every young girl loves to look at herself in the mirror, to try different hairdos, secretly to put on her mother's makeup, jewelry, and shoes. I had never had a chance to do any of that. In the ghetto I had only been able to see my reflection in windows, but who wanted to look?

Immediately after the liberation, I saw myself in the mirror over the sink in the school at Kiel, and I had been horrified by what I had seen. A monster was looking out at me from that mirror, someone so ugly that I couldn't believe it was really me. I had never pictured myself as looking like the other women, emaciated and half-dead, though of course I was. My face was ravaged and I couldn't stand it. For days I avoided looking into the mirror, and then I would find myself staring obsessively at that stranger's face, trying to figure out how it could be my own.

Now, after two months of decent food and rest, I was starting to think of myself as pretty again. Did Manfred mainly see traces of my suffering, or did he see the promise of my youth? I didn't dare ask him.

Manfred had been sent to Dachau with the other men from the Kovno ghetto, and the story of his survival is as miraculous as the story of my mother's and mine, a combination of determination, faith, and impossible luck. After the American army liberated Dachau, Manfred went to

Frankfurt, because that had been his birthplace. Miraculously, Dita had also survived. Manfred and Dita began searching for each other, and, not long after the liberation, she also made her way to Frankfurt. After they were reunited, they broke into an apartment that had belonged to a Nazi who was either missing in action or in hiding to avoid being tried as a war criminal. There they set up house. Jews in Germany commonly did this whenever they could after the war. It was their way of getting revenge, and they also needed a place to live. No one dared say a word in protest. The Germans knew what they had done to us.

It must have been on that first visit to Frankfurt that we learned for certain that, before the Red Army liberated Kovno, the Nazis had burned everyone to death who had been left behind in the Kovno ghetto, including my mother's parents and her brother Jakob, who had been left alive in the ghetto after Benno was shot before his mother's eyes. The soldiers went from bunker to bunker with grenades and flamethrowers, systematically wiping out the small remnant of defenseless Jews who were hiding there, innocent, unarmed, weak civilians who constituted no threat whatsoever to the German war effort. We also learned that my aunt Tita and her husband had been killed in Riga. There was no one left for us to look for in the lists.

The second item on the refugees' agenda, after they had found their surviving relatives and learned the fate of those who hadn't survived, was to get out of Germany. Manfred and Dita planned to emigrate to America as soon as possible, and they wanted my mother and me to come with them. We had a number of cousins who had gone to

America from Germany before the war. As soon as they could, they located us through the Joint Distribution Committee and supplied affidavits so that we could emigrate to the United States. They expected we would be able to leave within a few months. The prospect was exciting. America, a country where dreams came true, a country untouched by the destruction of war—I couldn't wait to go!

Mother and I returned to Kiel after our reunion with Manfred, and once we were well enough the British sent us down to Feldafing, a pleasant resort town on the Starnbergersee, south of Munich. We were placed in modest apartments, where we waited for our American visas to come through. Meanwhile, we enjoyed the landscape and continued to receive medical treatment at the hospital in Feldafing. The field of medicine interested me so I started helping in the laboratory, getting informal training as a medical technician.

In Feldafing we were joined by one other surviving member of our family, my mother's cousin. After a month or so my mother decided she had to visit Manfred again, so she set out for Munich, leaving me with our cousin back in Feldafing. The trip from Munich to Frankfurt, which today would take only half a day or so by train or car, took over thirteen hours in the crowded, disrupted trains of 1945. It was an exhausting trip for a woman who had barely had time to recover from the suffering and diseases of the concentration camp, but Mother couldn't stay away. Naturally, I was worried about her, especially as travel wasn't safe at that time. The whole time my mother was away, one week, I could barely sleep.

Another survivor from Kovno had joined Manfred and Dita, a young man nicknamed "Wulik" (the Lithuanian equivalent of Bill). Dita had known Wulik in Kovno. When Wulik checked in at the relief organization in Frankfurt, Dita recognized him, and she invited him to share their flat.

Like Manfred, Wulik had also been imprisoned in Dachau, and after the liberation he stayed with the American Third Army, the unit that had been involved in liberating the concentration camp. He worked mainly as an interpreter, but occasionally he also helped out in the kitchen, where he won the odd nickname of "William Jam-and-Butter." It seems that once he was asked to serve butter and jam for breakfast. Being such an "experienced" cook, he stirred the two ingredients together in a big pot. The soldiers had been rather surprised when Wulik spooned that gooey mixture out onto their trays, but they ate it and enjoyed it. The soldiers and officers all liked "William Jam-and-Butter," and the commanding officer prepared all the papers necessary so that he could go to America as an immigrant when the unit was brought home. Wulik was the only member of his family to survive. His parents and brother had been killed in the ghetto. Nevertheless, the prospect of living in the United States never tempted him, and he always planned to go to Palestine, which was still under British rule.

Before the war Wulik had been an active Zionist, and he never forsook his ideals. He had been active in the anti-Nazi Zionist underground movement in the camps, and when he met Dita in Frankfurt he was actively involved with the smuggling of illegal immigrants from Europe to

Palestine, based on contacts he had made while serving with the American army on the border between Czechoslovakia and Russia.

Although he had settled in Frankfurt with Dita and Manfred, Wulik's duties took him all over Europe. He was working with the former soldiers of the Jewish Brigade and other emissaries from mandatory Palestine who had come to Europe and begun organizing the refugees for immigration to what was to become the State of Israel. Wulik began to use his Hebrew name, Zeev, and he actually spoke Hebrew better than many of the emissaries from mandatory Palestine, because he had graduated from the Hebrew Gymnasium in Kovno. In fact, when Ben-Gurion came to Europe to observe the work with refugees, he was so impressed by the way Zeev spoke Hebrew that he couldn't believe he had never been in Palestine.

My mother had not known Wulik in Kovno, but they got along very well from the start. He was a sensitive, intelligent, good-looking young man from a good family, with what we German Jews call *Kinderstube* (the nursery), meaning that he had been well brought up. He also admired her. She was an intelligent, refined, well educated woman who spoke fine German and always made sure she was well groomed, even so soon after the war. Unfortunately, she was losing the sight of one eye because of vitamin deficiency, and she was afraid the eye would have to be removed.

Mother had brought a photograph of me to Frankfurt to show Manfred, and when Zeev saw the picture, after having been so impressed by my mother, he resolved that I was the girl he was going to marry. Of course, he didn't let my mother or anyone else in on this secret plan of his, and I hadn't even met him yet. I didn't even know he existed!

Mother returned to Feldafing, but Manfred and Dita had begged her to send me to Frankfurt on a visit, so with my elderly cousin as a chaperone I took the long train ride back. Our plan was still that we would all go to America together as soon as the visas came through.

The train trip from Munich to Frankfurt took more than thirteen hours. It was a nightmare. The car was full of rowdy, drunken Germans. Which ones, I kept wondering, had been SS or Kapos? Which ones had murdered and beaten Jews and stolen their property?

Manfred was waiting for us on the platform at Frankfurt. I was wearing one of my two dresses, sent by my cousins in a parcel from America: it was a girlish, short dress, and I wore white knee-socks and black patent leather shoes. I also had grown a fashionable curl, known as a *Tolle*, over my forehead. But my eyes were badly infected, and my figure was a mess, still lumpy. I had also developed severe asthma. I coughed and wheezed all the time.

After Manfred finished greeting my cousin and me, he picked up my cousin's bundle and we started to leave the platform. However, unbeknownst to Manfred, Zeev was also waiting for us at the railroad station when I arrived from Feldafing. He kept out of view until we started climbing the steps with our bundles, and then he ambled down as if he just happened to be passing through at the moment of our arrival.

He greeted me gallantly: "Why hello, you must be

Manfred's sister, Trudi. I've seen your picture, and Manfred has told me so much about you. I'm delighted to meet you!" Zeev immediately took my bundle and started back up the steps with us.

My first impression of Zeev was quite favorable. He was very thin, with dark hair and brown, intelligent eyes. Although he was wearing the simplest of clothing, he had a dignified air about him. He was self-confident without being brash, and I could see right away that he was a good person, a person one could trust. Despite everything he had gone through, his behavior showed he was cultivated and well brought up. Clearly, he was also a very strong-willed, determined person. Before we reached the top of the steps he had announced that I was going to move to Palestine with him. I thought he was out of his mind.

After an enjoyable week in Frankfurt, I returned to Feldafing and continued my informal studies in the hospital. The doctors and nurses were kind to me and glad to teach me how to work in the laboratory, but they kept asking me why I never smiled. "You're bright and young, but you're so gloomy."

I told them simply, "I've got such terrible memories."

How could I explain that the only smiles that had been on my face during the past four years had been false smiles, smiles to ingratiate myself with the Nazis?

Zeev visited me often in Feldafing. He had to travel a great deal for his work, which was semiclandestine. He went from one displaced-persons camp to another. He organized groups of young Jews and helped prepare them for immigration to the Land of Israel. Instructors were sent from Palestine to teach the refugees Hebrew, Israeli folk songs, and self-defense, but the main point was to get them moving south to Mediterranean ports. The Jewish Agency chartered ships to spirit the refugees into Palestine against the will of the British government, which preferred to see Hitler's victims rot in Europe than help them join their fellow Jews in the Land of Israel and begin a new life.

Whenever Zeev came to Feldafing we spent time together. I was beginning to enjoy his company very much. I also missed him and worried about him when he was gone. His work had an element of danger. One could never tell when hooligans might decide to attack a Jew, despite everything that had already been done to us.

One afternoon someone knocked on the door of our little apartment in Feldafing and asked for me in German. Only my mother and I were home at the time. My first thought was that it might be someone with a message from Zeev, or—a flash of fear zipped through my mind— perhaps there was bad news. Fortunately, it was not a messenger with bad news. What followed was one of the oddest scenes I've ever lived through, one that has left an indelible memory in me.

I opened the door and there stood a tall, thin man with brown hair, blue eyes, and a "Jewish" nose. He looked very familiar to me, but I couldn't place him at first. He could tell by my expression that I was bewildered, so he said, "Don't you remember me, Trudi?"

The moment I heard his voice everything flooded back with a rush. It was Axel Benz, the German soldier who had befriended and protected me while escorting the marches to work from the Kovno ghetto, the one who had given me his gold watch.

I had never expected to see him again. I had met or known countless people during the war, most of whom I knew I would never see again. They inhabited a separate and distant compartment of my memory, an area I seldom visited because it was too full of pain. Now Benz had emerged from that region, safe and sound. I was very pleased to see him.

"Would you like to come on a walk with me?" he asked. "We'll have a cup of coffee together."

I couldn't accept his invitation. I would have been embarrassed to be seen in public with a German man. "No," I said. "You may come in here. Please, sit down." I pointed to a straight chair next to the dining room table, and Benz sat down.

"Would you like something to eat or drink?"

"Oh, no, I couldn't take anything from you."

"It's okay. We have plenty of food now."

Benz sat down. I started some water boiling for tea and joined him at the table. "How did you find me?" I asked. There were always a million questions to put to anyone who had survived the war. Perhaps I should have asked, "Why did you find me?" or "What happened to you after they sent you away from Kovno?" But I didn't really want to find out anything about someone who had been on my mortal enemy's side.

Benz told me his story without my asking. His unit had been sent to the Russian front from Kovno in 1943. Almost all of his comrades had been killed or captured by the Russians.

Good, I thought to myself. They deserved it. If only more German soldiers had been killed, the war might have ended sooner. But suppose Benz had died in combat? This was too confusing. Benz wasn't an evil man. He had been kind to me, and I'd never seen him be cruel to anyone. Not all the German soldiers had been hardened criminals. I knew that, but their suffering was nothing compared to that of the Jews. My mind and heart recoiled from feeling sorry for the men whom Benz mourned.

"I kept looking for your name on the lists of refugees," Benz went on. "I remembered you so well from Kovno, and I prayed so hard that you had been saved. Finally I saw your name, and I came specially from Cologne to see you. Perhaps my prayers helped you, who knows?"

Benz asked me a lot of questions about what had happened to me since he'd last seen me in Kovno, and he was heartbroken to hear the unspeakable crimes the Germans had committed against us. He wept openly and said, "I'm ashamed of my country, so ashamed."

Then he told me he was engaged to marry an Italian girl. He loved her, but he wasn't sure he could go through with the wedding.

"Why not?" I asked.

"Because I want to marry you, Trudi," he said.

I was too astonished to respond. That was the last thing in the world I'd ever expected. It was so farfetched I almost laughed out loud. But I saw that he was deeply earnest, so I had to respond seriously. I hesitated for a long time. I didn't know where to begin. Finally I told him, "I could never marry a German after what the German people have done to the Jews."

"I'll convert to Judaism and emigrate to Palestine!" he said. I couldn't believe my ears. That was entirely out of the question. He could never make himself into a Jew. Everyone would immediately recognize him as a German, a former member of the Nazi army. I would be embarrassed to be seen in the street with him, let alone be married to him.

He was a sensitive, artistic person, and he had kept me company day after day on my dreary march from the Kovno ghetto to the military hospital. His friendship, which he expressed at great risk to his own life, had given me strength and courage to go on. He had reassured me that the war would be over, and, in his most generous gesture of all, he had given me his gold watch, hoping it would help to keep me alive, though in fact I had almost been killed when I traded it for food.

At the time he had said, "I hope we meet again," and I had tears in my eyes when he was transferred away from Kovno. Who would protect me?

Now Benz had appeared again. I remembered all my gratitude to him, and I was very moved by his impulsive proposal, but I couldn't possibly accept.

"Please, this is ridiculous. You don't even know me. I certainly don't know you. You can't propose marriage out of the blue like that! Anyway, I'm just a young girl. I don't plan to get married until I've completed my education."

"But I do know you. I remember you so well from the Kovno ghetto, how cheerful you were even when you were suffering. Such a sweet little girl you were!"

"Please, forgive me for being blunt. Forget it. You've built up a memory in your mind and fallen in love with it.

You're trying to make up for what your country did with a personal gesture. I understand that. But . . . "

Suddenly he got up from the table. He paced round and round the room in great agitation. Then he said, "I see I've been making a fool of myself. Please forgive me. I'll leave now. Farewell!" He walked to the door.

I stopped him. "Are you going back to Cologne?"

"Yes, why?"

"I have a letter for a friend in Frankfurt. If you could mail it on your way, I'd appreciate it."

"If it's for your boyfriend," he said, "I don't want to take it." But he did.

Axel Benz was an artist. When I actually did get married, he sent me a beautiful painting of his, a large landscape of a German village. It is hanging in my apartment in Jerusalem to this day, though I've completely lost contact with Benz.

Axel Benz wasn't the only one who placed demands on my future. Our American visas were due to come through, and Manfred and Dita were arranging passage for us. But Zeev kept pressuring us to go to Palestine. That was the country for a Jewish person. Zeev also wanted to marry me, but I wasn't ready to accept his proposal yet. I wasn't in a hurry to form a permanent attachment to anyone. I hardly knew what love was at the time. I was totally inexperienced in personal relationships, except for my love for my father, which had ended in bereavement, and my deep tie with my mother, which had developed under abnormally stressful circumstances. During the war I hadn't had a chance to develop like a normal teenage girl, with friends and a life of my own. Even Manfred, my brother, had become almost a stranger during the ghetto years because he had struck out on his own. I felt like a very young girl. The five years of the war were simply canceled out of my life. They hadn't contributed to my mature development. Who could think of falling in love under those circumstances? It was out of the question. Zeev was persistent, but I would hear nothing of the idea of marriage.

Then something happened that influenced the course that our lives would later take. In early 1946, Manfred and Dita managed to book passage for America, but my mother and I still hadn't made the final arrangements. Our visas had not yet come through. Manfred and Dita sailed away, and we moved into their apartment in Frankfurt, bringing the scant belongings we had managed to gather since the liberation, a small bundle of secondhand clothing.

Once we were in Frankfurt, we suddenly weren't entirely sure we would go to America to join Manfred and Dita. Zeev used to speak so enthusiastically about Palestine that we were half-convinced to go there. This decision was far from easy. Mother and I discussed it for hours and hours. Manfred and Dita were anxious for us to come with them, and naturally, my mother and I didn't want to be separated from our closest surviving relative. We got along very well with Dita, and Mother would want to be close to her grandchildren when they were born.

As much as we liked Zeev personally, the main argument against going to America with Manfred and Dita was really more ideological than personal. Where should a Jew live after what the Gentiles had done to us during the war?

It was obvious to us that we had to leave Germany, and the sooner the better, though some of the refugees planned to remain there. How, I still wonder, could a Jewish person stay and live in Germany? It's not normal. The place for a survivor is not Germany. I can't understand that. What does a Jew have to look for in Germany?

Zeev was an ardent Zionist, and his arguments were convincing. Unlike him, I had never been in a Zionist youth movement, so I didn't share his ideological background. On the other hand, my mother and I were very sympathetic to his ideas. Mother had been active on behalf of Zionism in Frankfurt. She had raised money for the Jewish National Fund, and if it hadn't been for her heart condition (my father had been concerned about the hot climate), my parents would have considered moving to Palestine in the mid-1930s after being driven out of Germany. Still, all that was water under the bridge, and the arguments were far from theoretical. We had to make up our minds about the future.

We spent a lot of time weighing the pros and cons. Our closest relatives had gone to America. But was it the right place for us, too? Would we be better off and safer there? We knew that America had come through the war virtually unscathed. We had no doubt that, materially speaking, life would be easier for us in America. Yet we also remembered that the Jews of Germany had felt at home and prospered there before the rise of the Nazis. America might be good to the Jews, but Palestine was the Jewish homeland. Its future, however, was in doubt. This was before the United Nations partition decision of November 1947 and the Israeli declaration of independence in May 1948. And, naturally, we did not realize that the Jewish state would have to fight so often for its survival.

Ultimately, it was Zeev who swayed us. He convinced us that Jews should live in their own land, not as strangers in another country, even one that had been as good to the Jews as had the United States. We decided to turn down the American visas. When he heard the news, Manfred thought we were out of our minds, and I suspect he was angry at us for turning down the visas. Meanwhile, Zeev hadn't yet convinced me to marry him, but my mother and I had both become very attached to him.

We were living a disorganized, almost crazy life in Frankfurt, with little or no framework or aim. The Jewish welfare organization distributed cigarettes and other supplies, and we used to trade what we didn't need for food and goods.

Although the once-mighty Germans were defeated and living under Allied occupation, we Jews didn't have a feeling of victory. We had lost too many and too much. Many of us burned with a desire to take revenge. But as much as I hated the Germans and regarded them all as former SS men, I couldn't take violent revenge against them. That wasn't my direction.

I also was still frightened of the Germans, and I hated them both for what they had done and for their hypocritical protestations of innocence after the war. Suddenly nobody knew anything about what those wicked Nazis had done. However, I happened to find out, in a very strange way, that some Germans truly hadn't known the full truth about the horrible crimes which had been committed in their names.

A lot of my time in Frankfurt was spent getting medical treatment. My wounded leg had partially healed, but it still wasn't strong, and I walked with a bad limp. My tuberculosis also wasn't fully cured, and I had been receiving calcium injections for it. Then a cyst developed in my back, and I had to have a minor operation. That prospect frightened me very much because of the painful operations I had undergone in the Stutthof concentration camp. There, at least, the doctors had been Jewish. But this was Germany. The doctors and nurses would be German. I was not happy about that.

The operation was supposed to be a simple, routine procedure, though I had to be anesthetized. During the operation my mother waited outside the operating room, and Zeev kept her company. Suddenly the nurses ran out of the operating room, shouting and screaming: "It's too terrible, it's too awful. How did it happen? How did it happen?"

My mother and Zeev were petrified. They thought I had died on the operating table. Zeev cried, "What happened to her?" They heard him from inside the operating room and shouted back, "Don't worry. She's all right." The nurses recovered their composure and returned to the operating room, and in a short time they successfully finished removing the cyst.

Afterward we learned that under the influence of the anesthetic, while I was half-conscious, I had started talking about the horrors of the camps and the ghetto. The nurses had been too upset to stay in the room. Only the doctor had stayed, because he was in the middle of the procedure and couldn't leave. Later, while I was recovering, he came to me and literally begged forgiveness on his knees for what the Germans had done to me. He visited me twice a day and brought me flowers. But it was hard for me to accept those flowers from him.

At the time, I wasn't willing to forgive the Germans. I wanted to leave the country as soon as possible. I couldn't imagine that the day would ever come when I would be willing to travel to Germany and meet Germans, though I could pardon certain individuals whom I knew to be innocent themselves, such as Axel Benz or the doctor who had operated on my cyst and had begged my forgiveness.

My mother made a marvelous recovery after the liberation, and she never fell into a depression, despite her deep grief. All her strength of character came out as she faced the task of making a new life at an age when, under normal circumstances, she might have expected to be living at ease and consolidating her gains while her children grew up.

Despite her health problems, my mother faced the future courageously. Along with tuberculosis, the camps left my mother with a severe handicap. The sight in one eye became progressively weaker because of vitamin deficiencies, and finally the eye went blind and had to be removed. She got a glass eye but not one of the best quality, and people noticed it. This troubled my mother greatly, because of her concern for her appearance. Until her dying day she was always careful to be well groomed and well dressed, in the best taste she could afford without being extravagant or showy. She was a lady through and through.

We had absolutely no money or property, so among Mother's first concerns was to make sure I acquired a profession. Because I had shown an interest in the medical laboratory at Feldafing, we decided that I would enroll in the Paul Ehrlich Institut in Frankfurt and continue my studies to become a laboratory technician.

I found my studies extremely difficult: the war had prevented me from going much beyond elementary school, and it was also very unpleasant for me to study with German teachers and rub shoulders with German students after living through the camps. I am naturally a sociable person, but I refused to make any friends at the institute. Every day I came home to my mother immediately after my last class.

The months went by, and Zeev kept asking me when we were going to announce my engagement. He was always a gentleman. There was no question that I enjoyed his company. When he was off on his missions, I missed him and worried about him, and I was very proud of the work he was doing: organizing Jewish immigration to mandatory Palestine. Europe was full of homeless Jews, people who had lost everything and everybody in the war, people who had no place to return to. How could you send a Jew back to Poland, the Ukraine, Lithuania, or almost any other country in Europe after the Gentiles had helped the Germans kill the Jews with such enthusiasm? Every square centimeter of Europe was soaked with Jewish blood. The earth was one huge Jewish grave. The winds were full of our ashes.

The only place in the world that was anxious to take in all those Jewish refugees was the Jewish settlement in Palestine, and the British had bowed to Arab pressure and closed the gates of Palestine. In these tragic circumstances, Zeev and the other devoted young workers for the underground immigration movement were not only saving lives and giving people a future, but they were also building up the emerging Jewish state. I was excited to be involved in such an important enterprise, even if only as Zeev's friend and occasional helper.

I was in a quandary because of Zeev's insistent proposals of marriage. I would discuss everything with my mother. "What shall I tell Zeev? What should I do? I like him too much to hurt his feelings, but I don't know whether I'm ready to get married. What would you do in my place?"

My mother listened carefully and took a long time to answer. "If you really want my opinion, I would say that you're much too young to consider marriage." She looked at me to see how I would react.

"I feel the same way. My childhood was cut short. Sometimes I feel as if I'm still only eleven or twelve. Five years went by, but they didn't count. They didn't add anything to me. I have to catch up with life."

"You're right. You need to live, enjoy yourself, develop. It's too early to take on the responsibility of marriage. Even under normal circumstances, if your father were still alive and there hadn't been a war, you'd be too young to marry. But now, since you've lost everyone, and your father can't help you out at all, how can you think of marriage?"

"You're right. That's what I'll tell Zeev. Let's wait a few years."

But when I tried to talk sensibly with Zeev, that reasonable man wouldn't listen to reason. He only had one argument: "I love you, Trudi. I know I'm going to marry you. So why put it off?"

"But you don't have any profession. We have to save up money before we get married."

That was a sore point. Zeev was thinking about studying engineering, but he didn't want to stay in Germany any longer than he had to, and his work for the illegal immigration movement was taking all his time and energy. He felt duty-bound to continue with that as long as was necessary. But he knew my mother well and respected her. What Jewish mother from a background like hers doesn't dream that her daughter will marry a lawyer or a doctor, someone with status and a secure future? Zeev shared my mother's values. He wanted to be able to support his wife and family properly.

On the other hand, my mother liked and admired Zeev. She used to say he was from *eine gute Wurzel* (a good root), and she was glad that I was seeing him and not someone unreliable, someone whose character had been destroyed by the camps. But she wanted me to have a chance to make something of myself. My mother made her opinion very clear when I asked her for advice, but she didn't intervene when it looked as though I wasn't going to take it. She was a very wise woman.

I was certain about one thing, and that was that I could only marry someone who had gone through the Holocaust. Otherwise my husband would never be able to understand me. Zeev and I understood each other perfectly. The more he spoke of marriage, the better it began to sound to me, and on June 1, 1946, we became engaged. I wrote to my brother and sister-in-law to announce our my engagement, and, impulsively, I also wrote to Axel Benz, who had sent me an announcement of his own wedding. Manfred and Dita and our American cousins sent us telegrams of congratulations, and Axel Benz sent me his painting. He wrote on it, "For Trudi Simon," and though Zeev was pleased by the beautiful gift he said, "He should have written, 'For Trudi Birger!' "

We were married on June 30, 1946, in the courtyard behind the apartment building where we were living in Frankfurt. Attendance at the ceremony was small, just a quorum of ten men for the prayers and a few other friends. Our apartment wasn't in a very good neighborhood, and all the Gentile neighbors watched the ceremony from their windows. I heard them saying, "*So ein kleines Kind geht heiraten!*" (Such a little child is getting married!). Who would have dreamt that after Hitler and his crimes, another Jewish wedding would ever be celebrated in Frankfurt?

Zeev and I didn't have a penny, and hardly any clothes. Even Zeev's only pair of pajamas was torn! But we did get to enjoy a honeymoon. My mother surprised us by arranging to have us stay in a rooming house in the Taunus for a week. The Taunus was still associated in my mind with that dreadful moment in my early childhood, when the Nazi soldiers nearly shot my whole family on our way back from a Sunday picnic. But Zeev and I had a marvelous week in the country. The landlady posted a little sign on our bedroom door, "Welcome, Mr. and Mrs. Birger," and I had a flash of recognition. That was the first time I really felt like "Mrs. Birger."

Every morning we started the day by picking baskets full of strawberries in the fields, and our landlady gave us thick cream to eat them with. There were also delicious cherries in the orchards. We picked as many as we could eat, and I used to come home with cherries draped over my ears instead of earrings. Now I buy cherries every year to celebrate our anniversary, but they never taste as luscious as those cherries did. A year had passed since our liberation, but we had been deprived of fresh fruit for so long, we were still starved for it.

Zeev's health had also been badly damaged in Dachau, and during our first year of marriage my mother helped to cure him by making sure he had plenty of fresh fruit and vegetables. We continued living together in the same apartment, and Zeev and I never had the slightest feeling that my mother was in the way. She and Zeev became very close, and she came almost to replace the mother he had lost in the Kovno ghetto. Zeev kept working and I kept studying, but you could say that for nearly two years we lived a life without any real structure. We didn't get attached to Frankfurt at all, because we knew we were leaving. Our life didn't get a solid framework until we moved to Israel.

Once we were married, there was no doubt about whether we would be going to Palestine. The only question was: When could we go? The British had restricted legal immigration to a mere trickle. They were intercepting boats full of illegal immigrants and detaining the refugees in camps on Cyprus. Meanwhile, Zeev was still active in the movement, and because he was so badly needed in Europe he couldn't get permission to emigrate himself.

Finally, in November 1947, we got permission to leave.

Strictly speaking, we were illegal immigrants, but the Jewish Agency was testing a new strategy with us. Instead of trying to run the British blockade and land on an isolated beach at night, like so many other boatloads of displaced persons, we had been provided with the identity papers of people from Palestine who had passed away, and we were to pretend we were on our way back home from a trip to Europe—though anyone could tell we were refugees simply by looking at us. Perhaps we could fool the British officials, or they might turn a blind eye to our obvious subterfuge.

We sailed on a yacht lent by the Rothschild family. Our conditions weren't exactly luxurious, and the vessel was very slow, but we were all in high spirits. What a difference between this voyage and that horrible trip which almost led to our death, in the barge in the Baltic Sea! On top of my tuberculosis I had suffered from asthma all the time I was in Germany, though I'd never had asthma as a child. Amazingly, it cleared up the moment I boarded the yacht. Also, for the first time in years, I laughed freely on that trip. We danced on the decks.

I had an especially good time on that trip. The Greek captain was a real ladies' man, and he took a shine to me. He was disappointed to find that I was married, but he was a gentleman and invited Zeev, my mother, and me to eat at the captain's table. He let me spend the day on the bridge, and he lent me a pair of binoculars. As we rode he pointed out the Greek islands, and I was as excited as a little girl.

The Rothschild yacht was seaworthy, but it wasn't as

fast as an ocean liner, and our trip lasted almost two weeks. During that whole time the enthusiastic atmosphere on the ship never flagged. We were crowded together and full of joy, singing Hebrew songs and making friendships which have lasted more than forty years.

The last evening of the trip, when the captain told us that we would sight land any minute, no one left the yacht's rail. We stood there for hours, staring at the dark horizon in hope of spotting the first glimmer of light from shore. Then, all of a sudden, in the middle of the night beneath the stars, someone made out the lights of the Carmel, the lights of Jewish homes and streets!

At last, after having been driven out of three countries, after losing home after home, we were within sight of a land of our own. I tingled all over, as though it were a dream, and I was much too excited to sleep. I stayed up all night and stared at those lights as, sailing painfully slowly, we approached the land. I wasn't at all apprehensive about what might greet me there. I was full of joyous hope.

We landed in Haifa on November 20, 1947. The new strategy of giving us forged identification papers was successful, and ours was the first immigration ship to arrive with no problem. We all kissed the earth when we arrived, something I hadn't planned to do or imagined myself doing, but when we first set foot in our homeland it seemed like the most natural thing in the world. Then I hugged Zeev and my mother tightly. This was the start of a new life!

Normal

CHAPTER SEVEN

My mother, Rosel Simon, passed away in 1981 after thirty-five fulfilling years in Israel. Upon her death, my husband and I lost our dearest companion. She was closely attached to our three sons, who were devoted to her. She knew Manfred and Dita's two children very well, and she also lived to see the birth of a great-grandchild, my son Doron's oldest daughter. It was a blow to all of us when she died. She had contributed to our happiness with her wisdom.

Mother's funeral was one of the most painful moments in my life after the liberation. I lost the capacity to smile for a year or more. All the terrible memories of the Holocaust flooded me, the agony and fear I had lived through with her. While Mother was alive, I used to talk about these dreadful things with her. Now I had no one with whom to share these memories. She had been my best friend while I was a girl in the ghetto because all my school friends were killed, and she was the only one who could fully understand the horror of what we had lived through together, moments such as the shooting of my uncle Benno before his mother's eyes. Mother knew the grief of returning home from degrading work in the military hospital and finding that my dear father, her beloved husband, had been taken away and shot. She had felt the gnawing fear that filled every day of our life together in the camps, dread that we might be separated from each other by death. Now that death had parted us, though I knew that my mother had lived for a long time after the war, I suffered from unbearable grief.

Life in the new State of Israel during the first years was far from easy and comfortable, but Mother never complained. She had not agreed to come to Israel simply because of Zeev and me. She was committed to living in Israel, and she loved the country. She became a dedicated Zionist and an enthusiastic patriot. She learned Hebrew, though far from perfectly, and the three of us helped each other start from zero and make a new life together. My mother shared our hardships cheerfully.

For the first few years after our immigration we remained in Haifa. Zeev and I shared a rented room with Mother. The two of us got jobs, and Mother baked cakes to make some extra money. We were content in that room. We had almost no possessions; the only things we had brought from Europe were some secondhand clothes our cousins had sent us in parcels from America, the painting Axel Benz had given us as a wedding present, and the cook's blood-stained blanket from the barge. But we didn't need a lot. We were so grateful to be alive that we had few demands.

Before the war my mother had filled our home with pretty things, but not a single one of them remained in our possession. She was never bitter about that loss, but to her dying day, she remained the lady she had been in Frankfurt, dressing with refined taste and dignity. She was always a great reader and was well informed about culture, ideas, and current events. She even began to play the piano again, once we could afford an instrument. My boys loved and admired her, enjoyed her company, and were proud of her.

Because of the bonds we formed in the ghetto and the camps, my mother and I always remained the closest companions imaginable. We understood each other perfectly. I could talk openly to her and get sound advice from her. She remained alert and open-minded to the end. Unfortunately, she was unable to move about freely during her last years. She fell and broke her hip, and it became infected. After that she had to use a walker, but she bore that pain and affliction, too, with characteristic courage.

Mother never complained, and neither did Zeev and I. We all worked very hard and made do with very little. What was important to us was to be together in our new homeland. However, the tensions and dangers of the War of Independence were not easy for my mother and me to bear. She was always worried about us, but she bore her anxiety very bravely. Once a bomb went off in downtown Haifa, not far from where Zeev and I were working. The sound of that explosion brought us both right back to the times when the Russians were shelling Stutthof. Mother was frantic. She couldn't stand the idea that I might fall victim to another bomb, so I agreed to work closer to our home, where terrorism was not so rife.

Zeev and I both served in the new Israeli army during the War of Independence. I was stationed in a military camp and worked as a lab technician, giving draftees blood tests, and Zeev served as a soldier. During the daytime I managed nicely, but I had very disturbing nightmares. Nighttime is always the hardest time for a survivor. The memories come flooding back, and nothing stands in their way. Once, during the War of Independence, I went to sleep in the army camp, and in the middle of night I woke up with horror, thinking I was back in the labor camp in Torun. The Kapos were about to take me out and beat me. My leg was infected. I shouted and screamed for help in German and Yiddish, waking everyone up. It took them a long time to calm me down and make me realize that I was safe and in Israel.

While we lived in Haifa, I often found myself looking out at the sea and thinking about my two ocean voyages: the grievous barge ride in the Baltic Sea, when every day I had expected my mother and I would be thrown into the icy water like the other half-dead *Mussulmen*, and our joyous trip to Israel, when I finally was able to smile again and the Greek captain was so kind to me and my family. I would stare out at the warm Mediterranean, but all I could see was the freezing waves around our sinking barge, and I almost found myself shouting "Shema Yisrael" again. I would stamp hard on the earth to remind myself that I had been saved, that I was in Israel.

After the War of Independence was over I wanted more than anything to have children, but I still had tuberculosis. In fact, new infections had broken out in my lungs. I was told that I couldn't give birth, and I was so heartbroken that I refused to accept that answer.

"Why not?" I asked the doctors. "Who would be in danger, me or the children?" When I learned that I, not my babies, would be in danger, I decided to go ahead. The risk was worth it to me. My first son, Doron, whose name means "gift," was born in 1951. The obstetrician who delivered Doron had known Zeev well in Dachau, and only his devoted care made it possible for me to have a normal birth rather than a caesarean section, so that later I was able to have two more boys, Oded and Gil.

Zeev and I tried not to raise our children under the shadow of the Holocaust. They know we are survivors, but we have never burdened them with all the gruesome details. Not that I ever felt ashamed in any way for being a Holocaust survivor; on the contrary, I always felt proud that I had made it through that hell.

My main goal was to be a regular, normal, supportive mother to our sons. I wanted them to admire their father and me as people, not to feel sorry for us as victims. Moreover, I never let the boys sense that my education had been interrupted. I always read a great deal and absorbed more than enough general knowledge to discuss their schoolwork with them and to offer them help when they needed it. I worked as a laboratory technician in various medical clinics for many years, and during that time I also took courses and earned the equivalent of a bachelor of science degree in microbiology.

I never returned to the strict, Orthodox Judaism of my youth. Perhaps I lost my religious faith when Father was murdered. I was angry at God for letting such a good, religious man be killed while he was trying to save innocent children. I looked for God, and often He wasn't there, though I have had the feeling that sometimes God did answer my prayers, such as on the barge in the Baltic Sea or when my mother miraculously recovered from dysentery after the war.

During the war, I found strength in a motto that I used

to repeat to myself in German: *Ein Schlag zu meiner Rechten, ein Schlag zu meiner Linken, nur triff mich nicht*—"a blow to my right, a blow to my left, just may it not strike me." It gave me courage, and, when I was strong enough, I was able to influence the people around me to keep up their strength, too. We had to show the Germans that we were strong, that we wouldn't fall down. In many cases we thought, "This is the end." But it wasn't the end.

The chances of survival were so poor, and the system was so murderously cruel, that anyone who survived did so by a miracle. But the miracle did not come only from the outside. It had to encounter some incredible reserve of force within the victim, who would recognize the miracle and become its partner. We had to fight off despair or else give up the ghost before redemption came. I always believed it wouldn't happen to me. I always hoped for rescue, and I was always angry at the world for keeping silent. How could it be that for such an agonizingly long time no one came to save us?

To this day part of me says, "Remove those five years from my life! Don't talk about them. Live in the present, for the future." That part of me wants to shake off these memories and run away from them. But I don't run away, because another part of me says that one mustn't flee from the past, that if I blot out the past, it will be an offense to the memory of other people who suffered, and to the huge majority who didn't survive. For that reason I have often spoken to groups of Israeli schoolchildren on Holocaust Memorial Day. I find it exhausting and painful to stand in front of a group and expose my sorrows. While I am speaking, I no longer see the young people in front of me. I see the ghetto and the camps. I see the *Mussulmen* and the corpses. And all the fear of those years fills me again. Yet as exhausting as this is, I continue to do it. I feel duty-bound to pass on the story of the Holocaust to the younger generation, while there are still survivors to tell it.

A few years ago in Jerusalem there was a meeting of Holocaust survivors. I heard about it and didn't think I would be interested. I decided not to attend. Yet some force drew me toward it, and I found myself there. And, once there, I was unable to leave. Nothing could tear me away. I ended up spending three full days at the conference, hardly going home at all.

I spent a lot of time just looking at the other survivors. I saw people walk in normally, but the minute they got in they started walking in twisted, tortured postures. Their backs curved, they pulled their arms up awkwardly against their bodies, and they began to limp. They held their heads at bizarre angles. They became what they had been forty years before.

There were signs for each ghetto and concentration camp, with lists of survivors. We gathered under the signs and looked for the names of people we had known. I didn't recognize any of the people from the Kovno ghetto or Stutthof who had come to the convention, but I did find the names of some girls who had been in my class at school in Kovno before the war. They were living in Australia. I thought to myself, "Thank God, they're alive." But I was unable to obtain their addresses so I could write to them.

Many survivors are paranoid; I'm "just" an insomniac.

It's not that I have nightmares; I simply don't sleep. I manage fine in daily life, but when a crisis comes—and life in Israel has been rich in crises—I say to myself, "I can't go on." During the Yom Kippur War, my husband and both my older sons were mobilized. I volunteered to work in hospitals. I knit stocking caps for soldiers, visited families of the wounded and bereaved—and all the time I felt I was on the verge of collapse myself. My son Oded, who was in the tank corps, took part in one of the bloodiest battles of the war, and the tension of knowing he was in such grave danger was almost more than I could bear. When I heard he had come through safely, it was as if I had survived the camps all over again.

I cannot face going to cemeteries, except to visit my mother's grave, which I do every Friday. Each time I go, I see the piles of emaciated corpses in Stutthof, friends of mine, my fellow Jews, who died horrible deaths. Almost worse than their death was the degradation that came before and after it. The Germans treated us like vermin before they killed us and like garbage once we had died. But we were human beings, worthy of respect.

One way I might have responded to that degradation, a way that a lot of people have chosen, would have been to make a "career" out of being a Holocaust survivor. I might have devoted my life to education about the Holocaust and to commemorative projects. As I mentioned, I have often spoken to groups of schoolchildren about my experiences, and I have also written this book, because I want people to remember the cruel things the Nazis did to the Jews.

Certainly, the work of commemoration is extremely

important. I have nothing but the highest respect for the devoted people who have built up Yad Va-Shem, the Holocaust memorial institution in Jerusalem, and other similar places in Israel and abroad. If they hadn't set about gathering documents, creating museums, and organizing educational programs, the Jewish people might have been tempted to let the Holocaust slip into oblivion. If we Jews had forgotten, Gentiles would have been only too glad to put it out of their minds. The terrible wound we suffered, which will probably never be fully healed, would have festered in shameful darkness, an evil secret lying in humankind's heart, breeding more evil. But for me, it would have been wrong to become a full-time spokeswoman for the victims of the Holocaust. I'm too much of a social activist.

You might say that the one way I'm not really "normal" is that I devote almost all my time to volunteer projects. The lesson I personally draw from the suffering that my family and I have endured is that we must work selflessly to help others. Perhaps it is because I saw such absolute degradation of human dignity that I now work so hard as a volunteer to help people make something of themselves.

I began working as a volunteer in the early 1950s, but when I was a young wife and mother I didn't have the time to devote to large-scale projects. I was busy bringing up my two older sons, holding down three part-time jobs (until I finally got a single full-time position) to make ends meet, keeping house, and getting the education I had missed as a girl.

After we moved to Jerusalem in 1965, while I was pregnant with my third son, I became involved with a program run by the B'nai B'rith organization to help immigrants from Oriental countries. The plan was that fifty women would each "adopt" a family in a Jerusalem neighborhood named Romema, where the social problems were dreadfully acute.

Right away I saw that I could do a lot to help. The women hadn't learned how to make proper use of the unfamiliar foods in the Israeli diet. I started helping them to plan their menus and to budget food expenses, and in many cases I saw to it that they had meat or chicken for Sabbath and holiday meals.

Many of the families needed the most basic things: beds, bedding, kerosene heaters, and clothing. I began to canvass stores and manufacturers, and I was able to persuade them to make contributions. I also started gathering used clothing from my friends. When I believe very strongly in something, I often can convince other people.

The families in Romema were extremely warm and responsive, and I rapidly became very attached to them. It might seem strange that a person with my background, from a middle-class European family, who had gone through the horrors of the ghetto and the camp, should have found it so easy to communicate with these people, so different from myself.

Perhaps the secret is that I never took a patronizing attitude toward the families. I never tried to narrow the distance between us artificially by pretending to be anyone other than who I really am, nor did I try to force the families to be anyone but who they really are. My human concern for their plight showed through the differences that separated us.

Soon I found myself spending all my free hours in Romema. The problems were so enormous, I simply couldn't neglect them. I would set out right from work and go from house to house, finding out what people needed and then getting others to help me supply those needs.

While I got ever more deeply involved with my adopted families, the other women who had originally begun working with me gradually gave up the project. They saw that the only way to make it succeed would be to work like me, night and day, tirelessly, and they simply didn't have the necessary devotion. "We're not social workers," they protested.

They had a point. Such a project can only succeed if it is well organized and run on a large scale. Individual efforts may be personally rewarding, but they only touch the surface of the problems. After working through B'nai B'rith for a couple of years, I decided to make the Romema project an independent one. I kept organizing, and I kept pushing.

First, as I said, we had to take care of some basic material needs. This was no simple task. Many of the families were squatting in Lifta, an abandoned Arab village at the foot of a bluff near the entrance to Jerusalem, where the roads were unpaved. One of "my" families lived down there, and the only running water in the whole house came from a faucet in the kitchen. The entire family, twelve people, had to wash at that one sink—of course there was no indoor toilet. The man of the house was a skilled construction worker, but he couldn't afford the cement, cinder blocks, tiles, and plumbing fixtures to build a bathroom for his family. Zeev and I found someone to contribute the materials, and we helped the man build what he needed. These people were anxious and able to help themselves, but they lacked the resources to begin. Once they had the resources, they made rapid progress.

Another key was education, an area where the parents couldn't help their children very much. They had had little formal education themselves. In many cases they couldn't afford schoolbooks, let alone the other books a child needs in the house to get a general background—encyclopedias, atlases, dictionaries, and books to read for pleasure.

To solve that problem I raised money and deposited it with a bookstore downtown, so that all the children on my list (more than three hundred) would be able to get the textbooks they needed—used, but up to date. I also had them all registered at the municipal library.

Then I had to make sure the children read the books. I required them to take a book out of the library and submit book reports to me every week. I also used to go from house to house and make sure that the children were doing their homework. Whenever I could, I visited the schools to see whether my charges were succeeding, and I went to parents' meetings with the children's mothers, to help them establish contact with the teachers and find out how their children were progressing. Finally, I had the older kids give lessons to the younger kids. My idea was that people who had received help should immediately begin helping others.

Despite all the tutoring and special attention, the children of Romema continued to do poorly on standardized intelligence tests, and high schools were reluctant to admit them. I had to negotiate with high school principals to persuade them to take the risk, promising that I personally would stand behind the kids. I'm proud to say that, in most cases, the children were successful. Many of the children of the families I "adopted" have gone on to finish high school or technical school, and some have taken bachelors and advanced degrees at the university.

However, I was only able to help children who were willing and able to accept responsibility for themselves. Romema is an area with serious social problems: crime, alcoholism, and drug addiction. I can only deal with children who have the inner strength to steer clear of these plagues. But when I see that a child is willing to make the effort, I do whatever I can.

Hardly a day passes that I don't meet one of the young people I knew as poor children on the streets of Jerusalem. Occasionally a policeman will see me parking my car and say, "Remember me, Trudi? I'll keep an eye on your car." Once, one of "my" children who had become a very dignified waiter in an expensive hotel coffee shop insisted on treating me to coffee and cake. I have received an award from the President of Israel as an outstanding volunteer, but the success of these young people is by far the most gratifying result of my work.

In the late 1970s, my husband and I had the opportunity to live in Paris for a few years, so we set out for Europe. I had had mixed feelings about going to Paris from the start, because my mother and our two elder sons stayed behind in Israel. Our eldest boy was already married, and the middle son was at the university. I was also very worried about my families in Romema. Who would take care of them while I was gone?

As a matter of fact, for the first half-year or so I was so concerned about my sons and my adopted families that I could hardly enjoy being in Paris. I got letters from the poor families every day. They were having one problem after another. I did what I could by mail, writing letters to school principals and other officials, but I knew that wasn't enough. I was desperate to continue helping them, even at a distance.

That's when I had two ideas.

I knew that many French Jews were from North Africa and the Middle East themselves, so I managed to persuade fifty French Sephardic Jewish families, not wealthy people by any means, to take on the responsibility of helping families back in Jerusalem. They began corresponding, sending money and used clothing, and also visiting the families when they made trips to Israel, and this connection has lasted for more than ten years.

My second idea has grown into a much more ambitious project. In my work with the poor families of Jerusalem, I soon saw that dental care was entirely beyond their means, and that they had all the wrong habits: they gave their children too many sweets in compensation for the hard life they lived, and they didn't teach their children to brush their teeth at all, let alone after every meal. Neither the Ministry of Health nor the country's health insurance programs had funds to provide dental care, so the children's teeth were simply rotting in their heads.

The only hope was volunteer dentists. But who? And

how? I knew that Israeli dentists, who spend at least a month in the army every year, would be unable to volunteer, but why not recruit volunteer dentists from abroad?

I started talking to people about my idea, and within a month or two I had enlisted six volunteer dentists from France. They agreed to come and work in Jerusalem during the summer of 1979. But where? My next problem was to find a place to house the clinic and to obtain and install the equipment. To make a long and intense story brief, I took a quick trip back to Israel in late 1978 to establish a nonprofit corporation to run my dental clinic. I also arranged to rent and renovate an old house. Upon returning to France, I persuaded a French dental supplier to donate twenty tons of the best equipment. Then I talked Zim, the Israeli shipping company, into transporting it for free. I cleared the equipment through customs with a personal guarantee that I had no way of backing at the time, and by the summer the clinic was in operation.

Since then, we have constantly expanded the pool of volunteer dentists, and today nine hundred dentists from nine different countries all pay their own way to Israel and work in our clinic for two-week shifts, some as often as every year, some even more often. Our patients are referred by the welfare office, and, of course, we treat both Jewish and Arab children. We require them to attend classes in dental hygiene as a condition for receiving treatment. Thousands of children have passed through our clinic by now.

Between the dental clinic and the Romema project, which has continued all this time, I keep intensely busy. Perhaps this is a way of compensating for the dreadful cruelty that was done to me when I was a girl. For I cannot forget it—not for one moment, no matter how my days are filled with fund-raising, public relations, administrative details, budgets, and meetings.

Every day something reminds me of the Holocaust. I am generally able to control myself; that is, I manage to control my behavior, but I can't control the images that possess my mind. I am haunted by pictures of the past. In dreams and daydreams I often see the military hospital building. It can happen when I use a public toilet. I suddenly see myself on my hands and knees, cleaning the filthy toilets in the hospital. Occasionally, I look at Axel Benz's painting, which hangs in our living room in Jerusalem, and I remember that one good heart among all our enemies. I still feel deeply grateful to him for giving me his watch at such great risk to himself. More than once it has happened that while Zeev and I are parking our car before a concert, I have looked up at the chimneys of the Hilton Hotel, which is next to the concert hall, and I think only about the crematorium at Stutthof. Afterward I can't hear the music at all. My ears are full of screams of terror and grief.

Sometimes I don't even know what triggers the memories. For example, the picture of the bridge into the Kovno ghetto won't leave my mind. I see those masses of people on that bridge, struggling to bring over their belongings. When I see them now, knowing what fate is in store for them, I want to shout to them, "Forget about your possessions! They won't help you! Find some way to flee if you can! Get away! Don't let the Germans kill you!" But they can't hear my warning, and it wouldn't have done any good if someone had stood on that bridge and warned us. In the summer of 1941 there was nowhere for a Jew under Nazi occupation to go.

The sight of a potato always reminds me of those times. I can still taste that watery, gritty potato soup they served us in the camps. How grateful I was whenever I found a bit of peel floating in it! I remember feeling unbelievably lucky, like a millionaire, if I found a raw potato in a field, even a mangled, rotten one—as long as some part of it was good—and managed to sneak it into the ghetto. I became an expert in potatoes, and I haven't forgotten that knowledge. Also, I can tell when I'm particularly anxious before I'm fully conscious of it, because I start buying huge amounts of bread and hoarding it. I still can't get used to the idea that a person can eat as much bread as he wants. And every time my husband or someone else asks me which way to drive home, I become the frightened little girl who was nearly shot by Nazis in 1934, because she told her father to take the scenic route home from a Sunday picnic in the Taunus.

These memories are so strong and oppressive that sometimes I wonder, What's the point of talking about them? Can anyone who hasn't lived through it begin to understand? It has given me some relief to write this book, though sometimes it has also been very painful. Before I started working on the book, my memories were very vivid and immediate, but when I started filling in the details, I found there were many terrible events that I had allowed myself to half forget. I had to relive those agonizing moments for the sake of the book. No matter what, long after any reader has closed this book and put it away, I will still be living with my pain and grief. When something happens to somebody else, it's dreadful. But when it happens to you, the pain dwells within you. You're alone with the suffering.

No one except another survivor of the Holocaust can ever fully understand what happened to us. These memories aren't part of our clothes, something we can take off and put in a closet. They're deep in our very skin! We can't slip out of them.

The Coauthor's Afterword

There are two voices in this book, one audible and one that
is meant to be inaudible: Trudi's voice and my own. Now,
only the second voice is speaking. You might say that I
have served as a medium for Trudi, allowing her to speak
through me in English. In no sense was this book written
by me for her, however. It was a full collaboration. Trudi
and I spoke together in Hebrew; though her English is
excellent, I thought she could speak more comfortably and
expressively in Hebrew. Before I wrote anything at all we
met once or twice a week for many months, and Trudi told
me her story. We didn't use a tape recorder. I took detailed
notes and prepared long lists of questions based on those
notes.

After gathering a great deal of material and assimilating
Trudi's story as fully as possible, I began writing, while at
the same time we continued to meet and talk. I tried to
translate our conversations into the form they would have
taken if Trudi could write English as well as she would like
to. Trudi would read through the drafts of the chapters,
make suggestions, correct errors, and fill in gaps. Then I
rewrote, and she went over the material again. We re-
peated the process until we were both satisfied. Meanwhile, we kept meeting to cover new ground.

Some of our meetings were harrowing, leaving both of
us exhausted, our eyes full of tears. There were times when

I felt remorseful for causing Trudi further pain by pressing her for details. At other times I sensed that our conversations were a great comfort to her. Their effect on me was paradoxical. I drew closer and closer to Trudi's experience, but the closer I drew, the further away I was, because I was constantly aware of the difference between hearing about what had happened to her and actually living through it. When I skip a meal, I get grouchy. What would it be like to live in constant hunger for years? When one of my children comes home late, I worry. What would it be like to worry about one's loved ones constantly, for years, knowing their lives were in fearful danger all the time?

Also, the technical process of writing often alienated me from the subject matter. I might write some harrowing sentence, such as "Two thousand children were shot by machine guns that day," and then I would have to stop myself and say, "Wait a minute, avoid the passive voice. Rephrase it: 'The Nazis machine-gunned two thousand children that day.' " Then I would worry about using an awkward verb like "machine-gunned." Was it justified to use a verbal barbarism to describe a barbarity? Finally, after fussing with the sentence until I was satisfied for the moment, I would stop myself and think about the meaning of the phrase "two thousand children." I visualized a huge swarm of two thousand children running around a gigantic school playground. I imagined the enormous noise two thousand lively children can make. I thought of the love two thousand children could evoke, the focus of their parents' concerns and hopes. I reflected that two thousand children are five hundred times my own beloved four children. Then I would remember that the Nazis killed more than a million Jewish children, and I would have to stop writing.

Over and over again I had to master my emotional reaction to the subject in order to write about it, although my purpose in writing is to evoke that emotional reaction in readers. It has been a difficult discipline.

Along with her harrowing experiences, Trudi has brought a strong sense of mission to the book. She was driven to get her story out, to honor the memory of the victims of the Holocaust by telling the story once again in their name. She also has a feel for the immediate drama of her story, a vision of herself, the young girl struggling against fearful powers, bolstered by her love for her mother. She dwells constantly in the immediacy of these memories. They are so much a part of her that she is unable to step back from them. I have tried to supply a more distant perspective.

With regard to the Holocaust, I am, fortunately, an outside observer. I was born on the safe shores of the New World when World War II was nearly over, and none of my close relatives had even remained in Europe to become a victim of the Nazis. Nor am I obsessed by the Holocaust. In helping Trudi tell her story, I have tried to preserve its intense, personal quality, but I have also tried to go beyond the meaning that Trudi's memories have for Trudi herself.

I have refrained from padding this book with information gleaned from outside reading and historical research. Nothing would have been easier to do, but our intention was not to present facts available elsewhere to students of the Holocaust. This book is based entirely on Trudi

Birger's personal memories, the memories of someone who was a child during World War II. It could be that some of the events as Trudi remembers them have been remembered differently by other survivors or documented differently in the archives and museums. Except occasionally to fill in a date, I have never "corrected" her version of the story to make it fit other published versions, though while writing I have referred to historical studies in order to understand the context of her story, and I often questioned her closely in response to my own outside reading.

The point of this book is not to state precisely how many people were murdered on precisely such a date. Trudi had no way of knowing such things during the war, and after the war she did not immerse herself in the historical study of the Holocaust. She got on with her life. But her memories continue to haunt her—and that is the essence of her story. The goal of this book is to convey what it is like to be someone who has undergone these gruesome and painful experiences.

The book that has come out of our work together is not the same one that would have emerged if someone else had collaborated with Trudi, or if she had written it by herself. Because of the nature of the material, our work together was occasionally painful and difficult, but on the balance our collaboration has been a pleasure. I have grown to respect and admire Trudi and I have become very fond of her. She trusted me not to distort or exploit her story. She also pressured me to finish and to get the book out. This was the main source of friction between us. Trudi's personality is powerful, and it is almost impossible to refuse her. But she is also an accomplished diplomat.

I met Trudi's brother, Manfred Simon, and his wife, Dita, when they came to Israel to celebrate Trudi's son's wedding. They were interested in Trudi's project, but I never interviewed them to fill out her story from their point of view. Trudi's husband, Zeev, has been sympathetic and helpful, but he did not wish to intrude on his wife's project. The testimony, therefore, is Trudi's alone.

Naturally, as we worked and thought about her experiences, Trudi's understanding of them changed. She saw things about herself that she hadn't understood, and these insights have become an important part of the book.

The main puzzle for me as I worked with Trudi was how she managed to retain such strength of character and integrity. According to what one reads about survivors of any mass catastrophe, perhaps the most dreadful and debilitative burden they bear is their irrational and obsessive feeling of guilt for remaining alive when so many others died. In contrast to those plagued by this survivor guilt, Trudi maintains an absolute conviction of her own personal innocence. I believe that she can do this more easily than an older victim of the Nazis because she was so young during the war. Moreover, because she regards the war years as somehow "out of time," unconnected with her normal development from child to adult, she has preserved the integrity of her character.

As I wrote this book with Trudi, I grew ever more aware that it is impossible to go beyond the words and share the experience of a Holocaust victim. One must feel more than prolonged physical pain, hunger, cold, fatigue, and constant fear; more than grief at losing people, places, and possessions; more than degradation, filth, humiliation, and more than being crowded closely with people one didn't choose—reduction to beyond the minimum. One must also remember that those who today are survivors could not, at the time, have known that they would survive. Further, one must understand what it's like to be the person who constantly remembers living through these horrors.

How is Trudi still marked by her experiences? She has deep scars on her right calf, but no number tattooed on her arm; at Stutthof they didn't do that. Her behavior is also marked: she is prone to sleeplessness, and the sound of a loudspeaker can put her right back in the Kovno ghetto. But not all of the effect is negative. The intense energy she invests in volunteer projects is also a legacy of the ghetto and the camps.

Today, Trudi Birger is a comfortable citizen of Jerusalem, wife, mother, and grandmother. But at night she remains little Trudi Simon, clinging to her mother for her life, and then helping her mother to stay alive.

Make books your companion
Let your bookshelf be your garden–
Judah Ibn Tibbon

to become a member –
to present a gift –

call 1 (800) 234-3151
or write:
The Jewish Publication Society
1930 Chestnut Street
Philadelphia, Pennsylvania 19103

A Jewish Tradition